AGING IS A FAMILY AFFAIR

"*Aging is a Family Affair* . . . is one of the most sensible, thought-provoking, detailed, and informative books written on this subject, to be found in any bookstore across Canada . . . It is written with love, nostalgia and true caring." – Ruth Bowiec, *Kenora Daily Miner and News*

"Illness can be anyone's tomorrow. With humour and respect, Wendy transforms a potentially painful crisis into an opportunity for creativity and joy." – Moyra Jones, *Consultant, Rehabilitation in Gerontology*

"The 1986 census indicates that 16% of those 75 and over live in long term care institutions. Family visiting according to the principles outlined in this book will surely add to their quality of life." – Dr. Gloria Gutman, *President, Canadian Association on Gerontology*

"Wendy Thompson addresses the problems faced by the institutionalized elderly, their families and friends." – Douglas Hill, *Toronto Globe & Mail*

". . . this is a book for families and friends of elderly persons, especially those faced with the responsibility of caring for them. It should also be a good reference for medical professionals, educators, students and volunteers who work, teach or spend time with the elderly." – Anne Thompson, *Daily Gazette, Colorado*

". . . Wendy has covered many significant areas relative to understanding aging and the aged . . . Her practical advice on several areas such as those related to vision, hearing, communication, etc. should prove very helpful to those who deal with elderly and/or handicapped or impaired persons." – Sister Roberta Freeman, *President, Providence Villa and Hospital, Scarborough, Ontario*

". . . the ultimate learning experience. Current research about aging and the elderly presented with clarity, passion and humour." – Sandra A. Cusack, *Consultant, Adult Program Development and Evaluation*

Dedication

To the loving memory of my father,
R.T.F. Thompson,
an extraordinary human being
whose illness and subsequent institutionalization
were the impetus and inspiration for this book.

Aging is a Family Affair:

A Guide to Quality Visiting Long Term Care Facilities and You

Wendy Thompson

NC PRESS LIMITED
TORONTO 1988

Cover Illustration: Marianne Dvorkin
Managing Editor: Janet Walker
Consulting Editor (Familybooks/Healthbooks): Dr. William Weiss

---

Canadian Cataloguing in Publication Data
Thompson, Wendy J.A.
Aging is a Family Affair

(FAMILYbooks)
2nd. ed. rev.
Bibliography: p.
ISBN 1-55021-029-7

1. Aged–Family relationships. 2. Aged–Institutional care. I. Title. II Series

HV1454.T56 1988 362.6'1 C88-094517-6

We would like to thank the Ontario Arts Council and the Canada Council for their assistance in the production of this book.

New Canada Publications, a division of NC Press Limited, Box 4010, Station A, Toronto, Ontario, Canada, M5W 1H8.

Distributed in the United States of America by NC Press Limited, 170 Broadway, Suite 201, New York, NY, 10038

Printed and bound in Canada

Contents

Acknowledgements

Most of all I want to thank my friend, **Nancy Dickie,** who patiently read every word of this manuscript, offering perceptive criticisms, gently pointing out unclear passages and helping me correct them. I am thankful for her friendship and her invaluable help.

To **Shelagh Nebocat,** social worker and editor of "Continuing Care Resources," I am grateful for her time and valuable suggestions. Several improvements in the manuscript resulted from her comments. My thanks go to **Jill Watt,** Registered Nurse, for her helpful advice and counsel whenever I needed them. I also want to express my appreciation to **Dr. Gloria Gutman,** Director, Gerontology Research Centre, Simon Fraser University, Burnaby, British Columbia, who has supported me and encouraged this project from the outset. And finally to my friends, who were very helpful as deadline time approached: Thank You.

Preface to the Second Edition

Would a five minute chat between us – with my coat still buttoned – add quality to your life? Caring for and visiting elderly relatives involves a myriad of issues that ultimately affect the quality of your life and the life of your elderly family member or friend. For some, involvement with an aging person is simply a duty, perhaps motivated by guilt, a burden to be endured. For others, it is a caregiving activity that involves immeasurable commitment, despite emotional and physical stress. For everyone, it *can* be a satisfying daily or weekly routine.

This book is written for the families and friends of our elderly population who live in their own homes, with relatives or in nursing homes. It is for professionals and caregivers, educators, students and volunteers who work, teach, or spend time with the elderly. This book is also for people who are contemplating the responsibilities of institutionalizing an aging relative. If you think you might grow old, then this book is also for you.

My experience in coping with aging started with a long distance phone call from my father's physician, some 1500 miles away. It began a new and unpredictable journey; painful, frustrating and devastating. My father was an extraordinary man, full of the zest of life, optimistic, generous, kind, an educator of the highest order, and a counsellor to all who knew and loved him. For many reasons (many still unknown), he decided to stop living. Since my mother could no longer cope with him at home, he had to move into a long-term care facility. Our visits were no longer happy times. My father lived for three more years–actually, he went on dying for three more years.

I sought answers from medical professionals, asked friends for help, seeking to understand some of the mysteries of aging. I wanted to alleviate my fears and most importantly to make our time together meaningful and enjoyable. As there was very little information then available, I determined to write this book. Researching it would help me find some answers, and writing it would help me confront my feelings of helplessness and hopelessness. I write it for those visiting an elderly person who are becoming worn out, frustrated and tired; and, I write it for those who just need a fresh outlook!

This book is the culmination of four years of scientific research and personal experience. The insights are drawn from visiting relatives and friends, elderly residents, professionals in the field of geriatric medicine, gerontology, educators, psychologists, chaplains and social workers.

This book will help alleviate some of the fears and stresses people experience. It will give you new ways of understanding your relationship with an elderly person. It will be an encouragement for those who shy away from our older people and institutionalized relatives and friends.

Professionals and lay people, alike, have found a wealth of constructive and creative ways to approach their relationships with the elderly. I have had thank you letters from families, phone calls from professional administrators and comments from participants in my workshops and lectures, that indicate the tremendous help people have had – the insights they have gained.

Most importantly, people have appreciated the positive approach of this book. Humour, creativity, and the need to communicate are as essential to this book as they are to life, old or young.

1
What is Aging All About?

BACKGROUND

How many of us give much serious thought to old age – including our own? Probably most would identify with Bernard Baruch's observation: "to me, old age is always fifteen years older than I am." The fact is, however, that one day, most of us will be old, and a knowledge of the aging process and its problems, will help us to better understand the elderly and ultimately ourselves.

In the year 2010, the first members of the baby boom generation (persons born between 1946 and 1961) will become senior citizens. Largely due to advances in medical science, life expectancy has steadily increased since 1900. Unfortunately, we have not added years to the part of life associated with energy, vigor and productivity, but rather to the last period of living, associated with physical and mental decline.

We must find positive solutions that will allow our aging population to continue to contribute to the society they have built and not be perceived as a burden.

Many of us follow the beauty ads, forcing ourselves to conform to the youthful ideal and then we marvel at our aging relatives still "going strong" at eighty-plus. It is more likely that our discussions center on the diminishing abilities of the elderly and their eventual need for around-the-clock care.

In this book, nursing home, long-term care facility, care facility and institution will be used synonymously. The elderly institutionalized person will be referred to as elderly relative, elderly spouse, elderly parent, elderly sibling, older person or resident depending on the situation. The term caregiver or main visitor refers to the person, usually a relative, who is the main contact between the elderly person and the institution. Caregiver does not mean professional care provider, but may be spouse, sister/brother, daughter/son, daughter/son-in-law, sister/brother-in-law, grandchild, cousin, niece/nephew. Gerontology, for those of you unfamiliar with the term, is the study of the aging process and the elderly.

A NEW ROLE IN SOCIETY

The prolonged aging process has created a unique role in our society – "visiting in institutions" – one that is often the major responsibility of one family member and which could, and most often does, continue for years. In the past few years we have had our consciousness raised concerning the special needs of the older members of our society. This does not, however, necessarily extend to the elderly living in institutions. It is this population which is of concern to me. Approximately 25% of persons over 65 will at *some point* in their lives reside in a long-term care facility, although in any given year approximately 7% of this age group lives in a care facility. Therefore, a much larger percentage of the population than previously thought will experience the difficulties and adjustments of having an institutionalized elderly relative.

From the moment we accept responsibility for an elderly person and make a commitment to be the "main visitor," numerous factors surface that will have an effect on our lives. Much has been done to prolong life, and many medical advances in health services and delivery are being directed to that end. We have added years to our life, *but* not life to our years. While we have little control over the length of our life, we have much to do with its quality. It is not enough to prolong life unless those added years can be meaningful and worth living.

May you live all the days of your life – Jonathan Swift

MAINTAINING FAMILY TIES

The most important part of a Nursing Home is the elderly resident. An especially important part of life for a resident is the family and friends who continue their relationship. With more and more people living into their seventies, eighties and nineties, there is an increased need for bridging the gap between institution life and life in the community. Adult children, spouses, siblings and grandchildren are part of the wide spectrum of age groups which are an essential resource to the aging population living in institutions. The age span of caregivers could be as great as sixty years, from a 20-year-old great-grandchild to a 95-year-old spouse or sibling. Your regular and concerned visits provide a major link to the community and help to maintain health and a sense of well-being. As you share your time with the elderly and increase their capacity to live more fully, you can also increase that capacity for yourself.

Maintaining family ties is very important to maintaining the well-being of the aged person. Spending time with the elderly helps meet the need for personal contact, contributes to the development of one's self image and self-worth by providing love, affection, approval and support, helps to establish a sense of belonging, and provides opportunity for sharing information and ideas that are essential for survival and life satisfaction. The elderly themselves say that a continuing tie with people (maintained through visits) is the most important contribution to their well-being.

Interestingly, there are similarities between long-term imprisonment and long-term care for the elderly. Prisoners say that loss of relationships with family and friends outside the walls, and the knowledge that "time waits for no man," were the most severe deprivations associated with long-term imprisonment. One prisoner said, "As the years pass, being away from your family doesn't get any easier, it gets harder." Some long-term inmates cauterise their relationships as a means of avoiding the anxiety and despair that accompany separation. Although this analogy of nursing home residents to prisoners may be far removed, both situations clearly illustrate the important issue of family contact. When and if family members withdraw their support and tire of visiting their institutionalized relative, is it any wonder that aged persons might also reject, (if only in their minds), the people they once held close.

Broken Family Ties: Although one of the main messages of this book is encouraging you to contribute to the quality of life of your elderly relative, some people for a variety of reasons, will not want to maintain any involvement in their elderly relative's life. Some family members may hand over their elderly relatives to the nursing home and have no more to do with them. For example, having alcoholic or abusive parents can be very good reasons for not visiting. The following excerpts illustrate the need that some people have to separate themselves from their older relatives.

In response to an earlier letter from her mother, a 40-year-old daughter had said that over the years her mother had called her every sort of name and continued to do so.

"However," she said, *"this letter is to inform you that I shall no longer have any contact with you. To make sure that you understand why*

I have made this decision, the reasons are as follows: you have denied my validity and integrity as a person; you have attempted to destroy my self-respect and belief in myself; you have undermined my emotional strength and stability; and, most importantly, you have shown me no love and understanding, even in moments of greatest crisis. In short, you have not been a mother to me for the last 23 years and I have reached the conclusion that you are both unwilling and unable to ever be a mother to me again." The daughter concluded:

"As you so consistently pointed out to me over the past twenty years, self-preservation is a basic law of life. Therefore, I will never again put myself in a position where you can devastate me emotionally. I want nothing whatever to do with you forever more. If you write to me, I will destroy the letter. If you call me, I will hang up. If you come to my house, I will refuse to see you."

Another person said it was a problem of treading a thin line between maintaining ties and separating from the family: *"It is hard to strike a happy medium [between offering too little or too much support]. I think I tried to 'help' too soon. My parents could have managed without me much longer and we would both have been happier."*

A 65-year-old woman had this to say about family ties: *"First and foremost there is a deep need by the parents to keep in contact with the child. At the same time, the child and the parent must each carry their own responsibilities, be independent, and each live his own life with his own interests and activities. [Parents should] become involved in groups outside the family so in later years when one is alone there will be groups of friends and individual close friends."* [1]

When family members can no longer visit or have decided to visit their elderly relatives only once or twice a year, volunteer visitors or paid companions might be used.

A healthy family life needs open and honest communication. Some conflicts are normal considering the age span between the generations. Close family ties can contribute to the well-being of older family members, but not if conflicts are left unresolved.

The last decade has brought new programs, additional and expanded services, all of which affect the quality of life, not only for the elderly, but also for you. Perhaps the most notable change during this period is recognition of the family as the major support of its own elderly members. The family as the major link between elderly residents and the community will undoubtedly continue. Those who remain connected to their elderly family members have a difficult and challenging task. In the chapters that follow, you will be given practical strategies that will help make your participation with the elderly richer and more fulfilling.

CHANGES IN THE LATER YEARS

Remember as now you pass me by,
As you are now so once was I;
As I am now so will you be,
Prepare dear friend to follow me.
– New England Tombstone

We're all going to be old someday, as someone once said, unless we die young. A knowledge both of the normal aging process and of some common problems of aging helps us to understand the elderly. It creates an awareness of how some aspects of aging affect our lives, in particular, our relationships and abilities to communicate and cope with our aging relatives and friends. Continual changes in the physical health of the elderly, alter the nature of the time we spend with the elderly. This means that we are going to have to make continual adjustments in the type of contact that we have with our elderly relatives.

They need to make continual adjustments to often extreme changes in their lives. Physical and mental changes, loss of spouse or family members, reduction of income, loss of home and community, friends and status, either all or in part, must be assimilated. Some elderly are afraid of old age, of being alone, of illness and of the process of dying. All of these factors piled on top of one another can be overwhelming to an elderly person who may be increasingly frail and vulnerable. We cannot predict the future, nor should we bury our heads in the sand. The best we can do is to try to gain a better picture of the aging process and to develop coping skills to prepare us for the future. Included here are some of the main physical changes and psychological challenges, any number of which, many elderly people are going to experience. Understanding these changes will allow us to adapt to the elderlys' needs and decrease our frustrations, while increasing the quality of time we spend with our elderly relatives.

The woman who wrote the following found some good aspects about growing old. Although the physical failings that come with aging are not to be taken lightly, levity can often be a great relief.

When I am an old woman I shall wear purple

When I am an old woman I shall wear purple
With a red hat which doesn't go, and doesn't suit me,
And I shall spend my pension on brandy and summer gloves
And satin sandals, and say we've no money for butter.
And I shall sit down on the pavement when I'm tired
And gobble up samples in shops and press alarm bells
And run my stick along the public railings
And make up for the sobriety of my youth.
I shall go out in my slippers in the rain
And pick the flowers in other people's gardens
And learn to spit.

You can wear terrible shirts and grow more fat

And eat three pounds of sausages at a go
Or only bread and pickle for a week
And hoard pens and pencils and beermats and things in boxes.

But meanwhile we must stay respectable
And must not shame the children; they mind more,
Even than we do, being noticeable.
We will keep dry with sensible clothes and spend
According to good value, and do what's best
To bring the best for us and our children.

But maybe I ought to practice a little now?
So people who know me will not be too shocked and surprised
When suddenly I am old, and start to wear purple.
– Author Unknown

Vision: Eyes are our windows to the world. Older persons often have difficulty reading and need more light to see properly. Glare can be reduced by sheer curtains. Physical changes occur: eyes become dryer, depth perception changes, night vision often declines. The ability to see objects clearly decreases and adaptation time from light to dark is increased. Greens and blues are difficult to see. Bright reds, yellows and oranges can be used for walls and rugs.

Things that can help:

1. Ask the nursing home staff about regular checkups.
2. Surgery
3. Glasses
4. Magnifying lenses
5. Environment – sufficient light, larger print, bold clear colors
6. Get information and help from the Blind Institute.
7. For more ideas see Chapter 7.

Common Causes of Visual Impairment: [2]

Visual impairment can be the result of an accident, a medical problem or be genetic in nature. Early diagnosis and treatment can often prevent blindness. Regular medical and eye checkups should be an ongoing part of your health care program. Some of the more common causes of visual impairment are:

Cataracts – This eye condition involves an opacity, or cloudiness in the lens of the eye, which results in a dimness of vision. Usually the cataract is removed and the individual is fitted with special glasses, contact lenses, or a lens implant.

Glaucoma – This disease results from a blockage in the circulatory system of the eye which cause the build-up of internal pressure on the optic nerve. Glaucoma has been called the "sneak thief of sight" because in its early stages there is no noticeable discomfort or visual loss. It only takes a few minutes to detect glaucoma by means of a simple test. When detected in time, glaucoma can be controlled with eye drops, drugs, or minor surgery. Otherwise, permanent loss of sight does result. A regular examination can help prevent serious sight loss.

Macular Degeneration – Although this eye disease can affect individuals of all ages, it is most often associated with elderly persons. Due to a breaking down of the macular area of the retina, clear central vision deteriorates, and the individual must depend on their peripheral or side vision. The actual cause is unknown, but the deterioration is associated with arteriosclerosis, aging, accidents, and systemic diseases such as diabetes. Eye glasses and low vision aids provide valuable assistance.

Diabetic Retinopathy – This ocular condition, which affects some diabetics, involves hemorrhaging in the retina of the eye. This bleeding results in distortion of vision and varying degrees of sight loss. It can sometimes be complicated by glaucoma or cataracts. Although there is no cure for this disease, laser beam treatments are used to help seal the blood vessels and reduce the chance of further bleeding.

Hearing: Hearing impairment in the elderly is known as presbycusis. It is not medically treatable and is caused by degenerative changes in the inner ear. These changes are most noticeable after 60 years of age and are manifested by difficulty in hearing high pitched sounds (s, th, f, sh, ch, z), difficulty discriminating sounds, and sensitivity to noise. Other causes of hearing impairment are working in a very noisy environment and heredity.

The inability to hear can result in unusual behavior such as irritability, fatigue, withdrawal, depression, anxiety, rudeness, speaking very loudly, appearing stupid.

How to Help:

1. Ask the Nursing Home staff about regular check-ups.
2. Hearing aids are available and are helpful to some elderly, but not all.
3. Have patience with the elderly person.
4. Ear wax should be removed by a doctor.
5. For more details see Chapter 7.

Sleep: With age our sleeping patterns tend to change. Older people may have difficulty falling asleep and may wake up more often during the night. The things that help people at any age to sleep – exercise, massage, hot drinks and regular bed time – will help an elderly person to sleep. Medication prescribed by a doctor is often necessary, as some elderly cannot get sufficient activity that leads to a natural sleep.

Unusual odors: At times urine and other body odors can make the elderly unpleasant to be near. If this is always the case, the Nursing Home staff should be informed. Some older persons become accustomed to the smells around them and may have a decrease in their sense of smell. As well, they may not have the opportunity to bathe as often as might be desirable. Offensive smells will bother you less with understanding. You may be able to assist your relative in taking a sponge bath.

HOW HEALTH PROBLEMS AFFECT YOUR TIME TOGETHER

> *We ought not to heap reproaches on old age, seeing that we all want to reach it.* – Bion

Chronic health problems and physical disabilities present another kind of crisis in the later years. Being disabled often limits participation in a variety of activities that can present a serious threat to mental health and the well-being of the institutionalized elderly. These health problems also create great anxiety in many relatives. They often feel it is their responsibility to motivate and challenge the elderly person "until death do us part." Hearing loss, a common physical disability among the elderly, hinders the quality of visits, as noted by many relatives.

"For one, I find it very difficult to talk to my mother because she has a hearing problem, and she is out of tune with everything. When we're talking I have to repeat what I say quite a few times, so I get very tired because I have to put a lot of force into my voice. If there are more than two people she cannot follow the conversation so she withdraws and gets very silent. She wears a hearing aid and it amplifies the background sounds overriding the close conversation. In a one-to-one situation she's fine, but more than that she's absolutely lost and feels cut off. Instead of her saying, "would you mind speaking up because I can't hear," she just completely withdraws. I've mentioned this several times and asked her why she doesn't say if she can't hear."

Another family relative experienced this problem in a different way and reported:

"Visiting in the room is tough because Dad's hard of hearing. You have to sit on the bed right beside him. It's difficult to visit in other places

because of all the interruptions. It takes so long to get to another room that by the time you move the visit would be over. Deafness creates huge difficulties. That's the biggest problem with visiting. Because he's deaf he does most of the talking. The conversation gets off track because he hears something other than what I've said. We're hoping his doctor will order a hearing aid."

For helpful suggestions on communicating with a hard of hearing person, see Chapter 7.

Diminishing Abilities: Some relatives of institutionalized elderly live through a series of stressful experiences from the time their elderly parents move into a Nursing Home until their deaths. The following example represents the views and feelings of many of the visiting relatives.

"I find it difficult to see my mother; for instance, I was there this morning. She has fallen several times lately and fractured her vertebrae again. She finds it difficult to move. She gets shooting pain in her back. I hate to see her suffer, but there is nothing I can do except try to be cheerful and that's not always easy. I have had her to my home many times and she seems to enjoy those visits. I used to pick her up in my car and drive her back. Until about six months ago she was able to walk here and walk back. She always enjoyed walking very much and if I could get her here more often and take her around in the car I think that would make her a lot happier. She complains a great deal and I understand that it is a sort of letting off steam on her part."

Another visiting relative put it this way: *"I think visiting is important because my Dad doesn't like to get out much any more. When he used to visit us in our home he'd stay for a lengthy period of time. But his physical condition is deteriorating and now the best place to visit is in his Home. Some people don't understand that even if you're just sitting there not saying very much it's still a visit. The most difficult part of visiting is seeing his physical problems. His bladder is not working properly and his clothes are often wet and smelly."*

Fears of Aging

> *To live with fear and not be afraid is the final test of maturity.*
> – Edward Weeks

Caregivers and visitors come face to face with the issue of their own mortality while they watch their elderly relative age and die. The following examples illustrate some of their fears.

Mrs. Dixon described her mother and spoke frankly of her own fears: *"My mother is still quite lucid, she's still very bright. The odd time she'll say, 'I don't remember my granddaughter's name.'"*

"I don't know how I would react if I was in there because I'm not ready for a Home like that and I think when you're changing, your outlook changes a little bit. I seem to find a lot of people who are very cheerful in the Home but they probably have been like that all of their lives and they manage quite well. My mother has always been very negative, there really is nothing in the Home that pleases her, so every time I come away from there I feel helpless. To think that perhaps I might have to go through the same thing. We come from a family where the members live a long time. My mother is eighty-two years old and she is very tired of living. I wonder if I had the means to help her out of this life would I dare do so. A friend of mine had lung cancer and then surgery. He was able to get something to end his life."

Mr. Hornby had shared a great deal with me about visiting his father, and as he was leaving, his voice changed from his formal business-like tone to one with a much more intimate ring. He looked right at me and said: *"It is something like prison life, isn't it? Most things are controlled – they tell you when to eat, when to sleep, even when to . . . I hope I 'go' quickly before my physical or mental ability declines to the extent that I need to be in here. Isn't it wretched to think that we'll be like 'this' some day?"*

Clearly, this was an honest response to the realities of institutional life. The fears of some day being in a similar situation, along with overwhelming feelings of helplessness and hopelessness, are experienced by many visitors. Feelings of hopelessness are not likely to change if our "hopes" are continually wrapped up in the expectation that things will be "as they used to" or "like the good old days." Similarly, if one continues hoping for improved health and better days to come, one will be sadly disillusioned. These are unrealistic expectations, ones that prevent us from accepting the harsh realities of institutionalized life. The vast majority of residents are not going to get "better" and go home, they are at the end of their days, months, and years.

The challenge for us is to forget that we or our elderly relatives are never going to decline. *We* are certainly going to change and experience many losses. And we are witnessing these in our elderly relatives. One of the best ways of coming to terms with these changes and losses is through a better understanding of the grieving process.

In this short life that only lasts an hour how much – how little – is within our power! – Emily Dickinson

Grieving Before and After a Death: Grief is an emotion associated with loss, usually a loss of something important to us. We can feel grief after a death, a divorce, the loss of a limb, the burning down of our home, or the separation from family and friends because of geographic relocation. Grieving is being aware of what we have lost, then adjusting our lives to the reality of that loss.

> *Friendship improves happiness, and abates misery, by doubling our joy, and dividing our grief.* – Addison

People go through the grieving process in different ways and at different rates. As well as the elderly residents themselves experiencing grief over their many losses, visiting relatives grieve, too. Some do not even know that they are grieving. The may feel they have failed when the elderly person has to go into a nursing home; they may become angry because they are frustrated about situations they cannot control. They may try to deny the reality of the situation. They may go through a period of bargaining with someone "up above" (for example, "Please let my father live until Jamie graduates"). Many relatives of the elderly become very depressed when they come to a realization of their loss. But finally we begin to experience acceptance. We begin to feel less burdened and to reconstruct our own lives.

Anticipatory Grief, Grief Before Death: The process of anticipatory or preparatory grieving is a difficult task. However, it often helps to work through feelings of anger and reactive depression that people may be unaware of experiencing. If elderly residents and their visiting relative can come to grips with their own mortality, they may be able to live a very different quality of life, knowing that death could come at any moment, but knowing also that they could have many months or even years to share. Although mourning an impending loss is necessary, it might well be a major inhibitor of healthy relationships and quality visiting between you and the elderly person.

Often as we watch someone we love age, become ill, lose physical and/or mental abilities, we are unprepared to deal with these changes. Possibly we project our own fears of aging onto the elderly person. These feelings are often profound and can have detrimental effects on our relationship with that person. An understanding of aging and of the grieving process, as well as of the feelings conjured up by an awareness of our own mortality, are important for improving the quality of the time we spend together with our elderly relatives. We don't have to say goodbye to someone who's still alive inside our heart.

Anticipatory grieving occurs as the relative observes changes, that they feel as losses, in an elderly loved one. It is normal to begin to grieve long before a health-impaired person dies. We grieve for the light-heartedness we used to know, for the things we used to do together, for what we never got around to doing and for the past that is now gone.

Things to do if you are grieving: Realize that grieving is normal and necessary. Allow yourself to feel sad and cry. Talk about your situation with people who will really listen. If this is not enough, go to a professional counsellor, your clergy or others. Get information and books on grieving and death. This will help you to come to terms with the inevitable. Try to keep involved in activities with others. Be good to yourself, treat yourself.

> *When one door of happiness closes another opens; but often we look so long at the closed door that we do not see the one which has been opened for us.* – Hellen Keller

2
Changing Roles

WOMAN IN THE MIDDLE

All Work, No Play? "Middle-Age," "Middlescence," "Mid-life Crises," "The Sandwich Generation" and "Woman in the Middle" are all terms that depict the group overlooked by our society until just recently. Middle years have been seen as a time of achievement, stability or power, but recently they are being regarded by some as years of mourning over lost youth, possible loss of sexuality, a time when, for the first time, one confronts mortality and impending old age, and years when one's own children are approaching maturity and becoming independent members of society. Another problem common to the middle-aged is their relationship with their own parents, who are old and in need of support and help, or who are becoming a concern. The increased numbers of people living to advanced old age has created new concerns and a new life task; one that does not as yet have clearly-defined guidelines or societal rules. Adult children are trying to define their responsibilities toward aging parents and trying to work out ways of dealing with situations for which they feel unprepared.

For the "Woman in the Middle" there are multiple issues, notwithstanding the "Man in the Middle," who, without question, has his own crises and problems. Many of the issues are experienced by both men and women; others are uniquely hers. The term "Woman in the Middle" refers to the generation of middle-aged women who are, in a sense, caught between their aging parents and their children, while attempting to be role models for enhancing the quality of life in both generations.

Because we now live longer, we are faced with multi-generational families, sometimes as many as four or five generations, and the family now looks within for help and support. Often the "Woman in the Middle" is caught in the dilemma of a three or four or five way split. She may have one or two children still living at home or the children may have recently left "the nest." At the same time, her parents, who have previously been independent, are reaching an age when they need her practical support or care. Even if they have not yet become dependent, an illness may occur and in many cases she may have her elderly parent or in-law living with her. In reality, she is more than a woman caught in the middle, she is struggling simultaneously with countless issues and crises.

Possibly a more appropriate term than "Sandwich Generation" would be what I refer to as the "Plywood Population." One's abilities and characteristics are used (or abused), chipped away or augmented before being compressed and molded. But the finished product has come out "good one side." Sometimes the pressure is all too great and a woman may simply decide to "split" – but not often.

Traditional Roles: Women have been traditionally trained from birth to be mothers and housewives. Nothing was more important than motherhood. Women were to be the nurturers and child-carers. Although the roles of women in today's society have changed (and modern families have also changed), that of caregiver remains. In addition to wife and mother, women are housekeepers, homemakers, career women, friends, family counsellors, family nurses, facilitators and parental caregivers.

One of a woman's main concerns is parent-caring. Concomitant with parent-caring are the strong feelings of obligation and commitment, whether or not the adult child has close emotional ties to an aging parent. It is important to realize that older people prefer to maintain their independence as long as they can, but when they need assistance they expect their children to assume that responsibility; the children, most often women, expect to and do take on much of the responsibility. Generally speaking, daughters and daughters-in-law provide the vast majority of services to the elderly. Even though women may not always agree with their parents, they still feel close to them and visit them often. When a parent is widowed, the greatest interaction and help is between daughters and widowed mothers.

The death or sickness of one aged spouse often leaves the other aged spouse in need of emotional support, financial advice and assistance, particularly in the case of aged widows who have never handled financial affairs. Therefore, this is also a time when a great deal of mutual decision-making takes place. Also, aged persons spend time putting their lives into perspective in preparation for their termination. They have grief work to do regarding the death or illness of a spouse and certainly about their own impending death, their own illnesses, and all of the losses that begin to pile up. Helping aged parents or other relatives progress through the last stage of life is often a time of great stress. Middle-aged women spend much of their time dealing with the needs, illnesses, funerals, and sorrows of their aging parents and other aging relatives. These women could certainly be termed facilitators, a role which in itself is not only extremely stressful but also enormously time-consuming.

The Youth-Beauty Syndrome: Many women in their middle years are struggling to accept their own aging process at the same time they are being confronted with the problems of their aging parents. Television, magazines and advertising everywhere emphasize the "Youth-Beauty" syndrome. Many divorced or widowed men in their thirties, forties, fifties and sixties marry younger women, hence the message, women cannot afford to be old or unattractive – women's wrinkles and grey hair are still taboo in our society. Recently I visited a childhood friend, whom I hadn't seen for some months. After a day of substitute teaching, she was preparing dinner for her husband and three children. Her extra income she said, was to "keep things together," not for added frills. Her husband arrived, greeted me with a warm, friendly smile and told me how terrific I looked. He then turned to his wife and said, "Why don't *you* polish your nails dear?" And she replied, "I barely have time to bite mine."

Menopause: Menopause creates stress for a woman. There are numerous biological changes which take place during this process. Her body gains weight or changes its fat distribution around the waist and hips making dieting and exercise necessary to maintain her figure, and she may search for more flattering youthful clothes. These physical changes have an effect on the psychological well-being of women. Some feel useless because they can no longer bear children. This obvious sign of aging can lead to depression in our youth-oriented society. She may feel she is no longer attractive, which in turn could affect her sex life. Some women react by drinking excessively, some seek out men who are loving and young, and some will isolate themselves to avoid social contact. There are, however, positive aspects to the physical changes that women encounter. As a result of no longer being afraid of pregnancy, having acquired more privacy with the children gone, and achieving a greater acceptance of their bodies, many post-menopausal women have a renewed interest in sexuality and better relations with their spouses.

The "Empty Nest" One crisis of middle-age, for some women, is the time when their children leave home. This time is called the "Empty Nest" or post-parental period. The children's leaving is a turning point for the family, a crisis in that each member, as well as the family as a whole, enters a period in which habits must change. Women need to re-examine their marital status, to renew relationships with their husbands and to establish new ways of relating to their children who are becoming adults. Their children are investing time and energy in others and in their own children, and this is difficult for some middle-aged adults. Even when the empty nest comes at the expected time, it takes a period of adjustment. This is a time to let go so that the parent-child tie can continue in a new way.

For other women, the "Empty Nest" is a time for establishing a less complex lifestyle and relaxing in the matter of child-rearing. This often results in changes in behavior, attitudes and relationships. Many women experience a new beginning, a time to set new goals, and look forward to this new gift of freedom. Depression from the empty nest occurs mainly in women who have invested all of their energies in the role of "mother." Because these mothers have had little or no awareness of their own egos they have not developed other roles or interests and need to begin searching. Many women resolve their feelings of emptiness when their children leave home by going back to school or beginning new careers. This new freedom often comes at a time when aging parents are starting to show signs of impending illness or are in need of special care and attention.

Women, once again, are faced with hard choices: this time the choice is between "gather ye rosebuds while ye may," and being a dutiful and devoted daughter while giving up much deserved freedom. Women faced with this mid-life decision need not make an either/or choice: the ideal is to find a healthy balance between the two. In the past few years the economic times have created yet another situation. The empty nest is beginning to fill up again as children are moving back home until they complete more education or the job market improves.

Middle-Age Affairs: Affairs are one common crisis of middle-age. Couples have had a long time to grow apart and they may feel trapped as they have a sense of their own mortality or a feeling of time running out. This often stimulates the urge to live-it-up one last time. Some women's identities and lives still lie in their marriages: often, if the marriage does collapse, so do the women.

The Labor Market: The realization of a woman's own aging often comes as a shock. Older women are at a great disadvantage in the labor market, competing for jobs against younger and better educated women, and younger men are promoted over their heads despite their competence.

What effects are women's careers outside the home going to have on their roles of caregivers to an elderly parent? We have yet to discover. One thing is clear: women are going to be less available as caregivers because they have changed their lifestyles and are entering the work force in greater numbers.

The Bottom Line: Old age brings about many changes in the relationships between parents and their children. The family network, as well as the wide variety of professionals who are becoming increasingly involved in the care of the elderly population, can share the responsibility of aging parents, thereby creating a caring community that can help turn years of loss into years of promise. Is it possible for us to shape a society which does not expect women to be "all things to all people"? The stresses for the "Woman in the Middle" may lead to periods of significant emotional and mental growth, and to the development of new interests and skills, all of which enhance her sense of self-worth and zest for living.

Middle-aged women have their own needs which must be recognized and met. Women will then be more able to meet their parents' and families' needs in a realistic and loving way.

A NEW ROLE FOR MEN: BEYOND MONEY AND ADVICE

> *Money* does *make all the difference. If you have two jobs and you're rich, you have diversified interests. If you have two jobs and you're poor, you're moonlighting.* – "Changing Times," **The Kiplinger Magazine**

> *Don't be troubled if the temptation to give advice is irresistible; the ability to ignore it is universal.* – Quoted in **Planned Security**

The traditional role of men, that of breadwinner, has changed in our society in recent times. We can see evidence of this in many areas. One of the main changes that has appeared in the home is that of men becoming caregivers to children, either as single parents or as house-husbands to working wives.

Studies in gerontology, however, show that women remain the principal caregivers. The man's role has been, and still is, mainly in providing financial support and in giving advice. But now, many men are the main contact with their elderly parents or aged spouses, and so must adapt to this unfamiliar (for them) aspect of care giving.

Maintaining family ties and being involved with one's own parents could be as natural a part of living as the fathering of one's own children and being a husband. Most of us did not go to school to learn how to parent (although it might have helped). Actually, during the past fifteen years or so, courses in Parenting are increasingly in vogue. Now it seems time that a new role, that of "Sonning," is ripe for development. Who taught anyone how to be a son?

We, as a society, however, teach our sons that it is important to be successful. "Go out there and get a good education, so that you can get a good job; get a good wife so that you can have a good family." And so on it goes – a good house, good car (or two) until finally we discover that someone tricked us. Much of this is really only an accumulation of material wealth. And then someone else came along and said this is what success really is:

> *To laugh often and love much; to win the respect of intelligent persons and the affection of children; to earn the approbation of honest critics and endure the betrayal of false friends; to appreciate beauty; to find the best in others; to give of one's self; to leave the world a bit better, whether by a healthy child, a garden patch or a redeemed social condition (our elderly population), to have played and laughed with enthusiasms and sung with exultation; to know even one life has breathed easier because you have lived – this is to have succeeded.*
>
> – Anonymous.

It is this definition of success that enables us to view things in a different way, ultimately leading to change. Here men will find some of the common themes that will help to bring them closer to an involvement with their elderly relatives.

I Simply Don't Have Enough Time: "My wife keeps in touch with my mother and visits her regularly, once a week in the Nursing Home. She tells me my mother is well looked after and we bring her home for dinner the last Sunday of every month."

It is true there is never enough time, if more time is really what is needed. Much has been written on the effective use of time. The important thing is to decide what is urgent and what really matters in life. The above definition of success helps put this into perspective.

What Can a Man Do to Help? There are numerous ways that a man can help his elderly relative: by being a planner, an advocate, by helping with transportation, sharing a craft, a hobby, or taking a walk. He can shop for and prepare meals for the "main" caregiver – his wife, sister, or mother. He can let his aging parent know he cares, he can do all of the things that women traditionally have done and still do. He can ask his wife or sister or daughter or daughter-in-law how he can help. Sharing the load makes for happier times for the whole family. One very meaningful and helpful thing that he can do is to say to the caregiver, "Thank you for visiting my mother, it means a lot to her and to me too; I know you do a lot for your father, he appreciates it and you make his life happier." By saying "thank you," he communicates his appreciation to the caregiver, an all-too-often forgotten message.

The following is a note from my uncle. It arrived shortly after a very difficult and stressful Christmas with my institutionalized father, and it meant more to me than anything else he could have done.

December 23rd, 1983

Wendy,

In haste.

Thank you for

- a. *looking after the arrangements for your Aunt*
- b. *looking after Xmas arrangements for your father and mother*
- c. *doing all that you have done and are doing re: your parents*
- d. *keeping open our family communications.*

Enjoy your Xmas to the extent possible in the circumstances.

Love,

U.D.

Climb Every Mountain: Some men, including many clergy, have "climbed" those unknown heights – the difficult places where we fear to tread – the personal places where we risk showing affection, saying Thank You, forgiving, making fresh beginnings. These are the "mountains" of life, overwhelming and scary but, once conquered, revealing a whole new world awaiting on the other side, one that can bring, amongst many other things, a greater meaning of life to an elderly parent and to you.

Turning an uncomfortable relationship into one that contains intimacy with our elderly parents requires great inner strength. Men can combine affection with a realistic understanding of an aging parent. Really listening to and really feeling the experiences of the old are abilities that when learned and practiced will change the quality of life for our elderly. Trite? I don't think so: that is the real challenge of our time.

Coaching Metaphor

Upon the fields of friendly strife
are sown the seeds that,
upon other fields, on other days,
will bear the fruits of victory.

Many coaches agree with these lines spoken by General Douglas MacArthur. You might hear them repeating these words to their teams. The strategies men use for coaching a young basketball team could very well apply to many other situations – most coaches have high expectations of themselves and of their players. The characteristics that these coaches demonstrate to their players – encouragement, support, praise, respect, affection, motivation – could be applied to relationships with elderly relatives.

The "game" is really never over, no matter what the scoreboard says. And the secret of the game is to "do your best." That's what the coach says, isn't it? It's not whether you win or lose it's how you play the game. And if a coach can make a man out of a boy – which is his real goal – then he has won the game. That's the coaching metaphor – using the characteristic of a coach – playing the game of life through to the natural end.

The Art of Adventure

A man practices the art of adventure when he heroically faces up to life . . . When he has the nerve to move out of life's shadows and venture forth into the deep . . . When he refuses to seek safe places and easy tasks and has, instead, the courage to wrestle with the toughest problems and difficulties . . . When he is un-

afraid of new ideas, new theories and new philosophies. . . When he considers life a constant quest for the noblest and best.
– Source unknown.

ADULT-CHILD/PARENT RELATIONSHIPS

A very few years ago we divided the elderly into two groups: "the young-old" (from 55 to 75) and the "old-old" (75+). Recently we have divided the elderly into three groups: the young-old (55 to 75), the middle-old (75 to 85) and the old-old (85+). These divisions indicate our new concerns. All of these elderly parents, at whatever age, and their children can be in critical stages of their lives, both groups having very different emotional and physical needs which are important and which must be met.

The middle generation has reached the time when they are reviewing their lives, evaluating aspirations while attempting to make some sense out of the accumulated mass of their material possessions. When this new searching begins, it is natural to turn to our parents for guidance, support and, at times, financial assistance. It is a painful awareness when we realize that it is our parents who need the support and care. At this point, caregivers often experience feelings of guilt or duty or obligation when attempting to come to grips with such questions as:

- How much time should I spend with my parents, my children, my spouse?
- What can I do for my parents that will make life easier for them?
- What do they really want or need or expect from me?
- What do I expect for myself?
- When and how are important decisions made for changing my parent's living arrangements?

Guilt, duty, obligation, responsibility, compassion – these words are often confused or used incorrectly. Webster's Dictionary says:

Guilt: the state of one who has committed an offense especially consciously; feeling of culpability; blameworthy, especially for imagined offenses or from a sense of inadequacy.

Duty: conduct due to parents and superiors; obligatory tasks, conduct, service, or functions that arise from one's position in life; a moral or legal obligation.

A CHECKLIST:
Things that family and friends can do for the caregiver

- Say thank you. Be creative: there are many ways of saying thank you.
- Ask what you can do to help, don't just jump in.
- Offer specific help, for example, shopping, yard work, banking.
- Send flowers as a supplement to your involvement, not as a substitute for it.
- Share the visiting, work out a schedule so that the caregiver can have a break.
- Invite the caregiver to dinner out after a difficult visit.
- Offer to send the caregiver on a weekend holiday – yes, money can buy happiness.
- Don't give advice unless it is asked for.
- Be supportive of decisions regarding your elderly relative.
- Read this book and discuss it with whomever was mean enough to give you this page.
- If you can't read, ask them to read it to you at bedtime.

Caregivers: please feel free to photocopy this page and tape it to a mirror. © Wendy Thompson. From: *Aging is A Family Affair,* reprinted with permission from the author.

Obligation: binding oneself, legally or morally, to a course of action (as by a promise or a vow).

Responsible:
1. able to answer for one's conduct and obligations, trustworthy.
2. able to choose for oneself between right and wrong.

Responsibility: the quality or state of being responsible as
1. moral, legal or mental accountability
2. reliability, trustworthiness

Compassion: sympathetic consciousness of others' distress, together with a desire to alleviate it.

These words can create nightmares for some people, so it's worth a few minutes to put them "in their place." For instance, if you feel guilty ask yourself "what offense have I consciously committed?" What are your imagined offenses? Hmm can't think of any . . . Ah, then what about feeling guilty from a sense of inadequacy? Most of us would not be able to find appropriate answers to these questions. Nonetheless, we still manage to carry around an unhealthy dose of this emotional poison as the account below illustrates.

The Past – Guilty or Not? Edna was a regular visitor. Her account of her feelings is a common story: past relationships and feelings of guilt have a great impact on the quality of visiting.

"I never did get along very well with my mother. I got along much better with my father, but my mother brought me up, she took care of the food and my shelter, my clothes, etc., but I never got any affection from her. She was too busy raising us, too busy trying to keep everything together. My father on the other hand I loved very much, however, very seldom did he contribute to our upbringing. I learned from my mother the niceties of life: how to set the table, to have flowers, good music and that sort of thing. My mother never allowed us to have the radio on, or leave papers around, so it was actually a loveless upbringing which has left scars on me and my brother. I visit because it's my duty. I don't feel I love her a great deal but I do have compassion toward her and I guess I feel guilty because she was the one who brought me up and I don't love her as I loved my father."

I asked Edna if there was any part of visiting that was "good." After a very long and thoughtful pause she described the following:

"Well, usually after I've told her the latest bits of news we can get into all kinds of memories and then we can sort of relax. She'll talk about things that are happening in the Home and if I start talking about the

past she seems to warm up. Of course, I have heard a lot of the stories many many times but just the same the reminiscing is the 'good' part."

"It is the last part of the visit when I'm leaving and have to say, 'Well, I have to go home now,' that's when I really feel guilty and get depressed because there isn't much I can do for her except visit her, look after her clothes and do a few little things for her. After some particularly depressing visits I walk home and make a point of looking up into the sky, up at the trees and see who is driving by instead of walking back sightless. That seems to get me out of my depression."

Edna's final thought: *"I don't know whether this is valid or not, perhaps I would feel less guilty if I could hug her more. This would help me and it would help her too. She is quite often the first one to give me a big hug. This is one area I could do something about, that is give her more love, more tenderness and more affection."*

People are most often unprepared for the feeling of anxiety, confusion and guilt they may experience because of their parents' difficulties. Often guilt feelings may lie deep inside of us and surface under the guise of compassion, caring, duty or responsibility. It seems that it is often through these words – duty, responsibility, guilt, obligation and compassion – that we define our feelings towards our aging parents or old people in general. What motivates you to help, look after and care about the elderly? Or what motivates you not to? What do we feel guilty about when we might not even know it? As in the case of Edna, many of us remind ourselves of our parents' sacrifices. They clothed and fed us, treated us to as much of the "good life" as they could afford; often they did without, or so we were told in order to treat us to a new, secondhand bike. They even managed to get exactly the right color. What a price some of us have paid for those years when we were "given to." And now it is our turn, isn't it? Our turn to sacrifice our time, our spouses, our children. This self-sacrificing behavior creates a great sense of obligation and bonds of guilt.

We can feel guilty over the most absurd notions. Some women actually feel guilty sleeping beside the nice warm bodies of their husbands because their widowed mothers are all alone. Your mother possibly prefers her new bed socks and heavy duty flannelette nightgown, although she'd never admit it. I can feel guilty about having a neck massage after spending a stressful weekend with my 79-year-old mother. She has never had a massage in her life and won't have one when offered although she suffers from the nagging pain of arthritis. I should feel guilty, shouldn't I? The power that guilt feelings have over us blocks the way to healthy relationships. If we were able to see clearly, we could know that we really have nothing to feel guilty about.

It is true that all of us are, to a degree, motivated by our own needs. If we *need* to please ourselves and others there can be unhappy consequences. Caring for parents because of guilty feelings, or other such negative motivations, is unhealthy. For example:

- People who feel guilty make unrealistic demands on others and expect them to do the same things they do, for example, visit as often etc;
- People who feel guilty may visit too often and stay too long;
- People who feel guilty may bring expensive gifts that aren't appropriate;
- People who feel guilty may not visit at all;
- People who feel guilty are often angry and direct their feelings toward other people.

It is important to evaluate our own motivations for doing what we do to help our parents. One way of doing that is to ask the question: Why am I doing such and such? For example, why do I phone my father every day? Why do I visit my mother three times a week? What is the motivation behind my action? If it is because of guilt feelings you might consider:

- That no one is perfect;
- That your spouse and children need you, too;
- That it is OK to make mistakes;
- That you don't have to be all things to all people;
- That your responsibilities to your aging parents may be fewer than you think;
- That your parents may not be expecting as much of you as you think;
- That you are doing the best you can, just as your parents did before you.

Too many people feel guilty for putting their elderly parent in a Nursing Home and feel uncertain as to whether or not they did the right thing. It must be remembered that your parent needed to be in a care facility, you did not "dump" him/her there. You did the best you could under the circumstances and you are still doing so.

Some adult children do have a deep sense of responsibility that motivates them to be helpful to their aging parents, however, some professionals claim that the present generation is motivated, largely, by agonizing feelings of guilt. Societal guilt, on the other hand, has resulted in the creation of service programs for the elderly, attempts at erasing stereotypes of the aged and raising retirement age. There is also an underlying belief that by helping old people we will eventually help ourselves in the future.

The Present – Who's "Parenting" Who?

Love while you have love to give
Live while you have life to live.
– Piet Heim

One of the best ways to help yourself feel better and to change the relationship with your aging parents is through group discussions. Some facilities have support groups for families. If they don't, perhaps they would be willing to start one with you. Listed here are some major topics that have been found to be of most concern to visiting relatives:

- improving communication;
- illness and confusion in the elderly;
- what to do together when visiting;
- information about aging;

Most of the topics of concern are dealt with in this book; however, there is no substitute for the positive effects of sharing. Often when major issues such as visiting patterns and feelings associated with visits have been confronted and dealt with through the group process, participants gain greater understanding of themselves and their parents or spouses. As well, they are better equipped to relate to their relatives, to help them, and to feel less guilty. Given new insights, it is likely that the valuable time they spend with their relative will be improved.

Basically, adult children live through a series of stressful experiences, not only during the initial adjustment period but throughout the total institutionalization of the parent. Caregiving could go on for many years. We owe it to ourselves to make the time we spend with our parents at the very least more tolerable, more enjoyable, and to strive for some mutual understanding and satisfaction.

Old people are not just like children, although some older people do demonstrate some behaviors that are childlike. There may also be a regression to childish behavior often as a result of the treatment they are receiving from caregivers, professional or otherwise. This behavior is not limited to children or old people. Some adults demonstrate behavior unsuitable to their age group, and although we do not recognize or admit our various tantrums, whining and manipulations, we often notice them in other adults.

Elderly people have had a lifetime of experience. After they enter a care facility, they will continue to struggle with adjustments to a new lifestyle. Not an easy task at age 78. You and I know very well what it was like to be a child, teenager, young adult and so forth. We do not know what it is like to be old. If childishness is one behavior that elderly people use to help cope, then we must adapt to it and try to understand it.

Elderly people need to be loved, not parented: they need to be treated as people who are adults, with experiences far beyond ours. The most important thing we bring to old people is our attitude; and they will sense yours. Older people, who at times may appear childlike, have the potential for growth and for offering much to the younger generation in terms of caring and sharing.

One goal for adult children could be to provide help to their aging parents without trying to control them. Too often adult children take on the role of parenting their parents. This role reversal is an unhealthy choice and will hinder the development of filial maturity (see the next section).

Old age is a time of many losses: physical, social, economic and vocational. It is therefore a time when adult children must help their aging parents to compensate to the maximum extent possible. This often takes great imagination and creativity. Building self esteem is a good place to start. Statements to aging parents such as you are effective, you count, you make a difference, you have an impact and you are important, are important for an old person to hear. Adult children can begin by talking about past and present capabilities of their aging parents in order to maintain their sense of dignity and self worth. Also, questions such as *What makes life worthwhile?* are no different for older than for younger people. *Will you help me with (whatever) like you used to?* Finding out what is still significant (a hobby, certain types of music, writing a story, what people still interest them). Make sure that you tell them they are important to you now and how they were in the past. Are there any new adventures they'd still like to experience? These are all the spices of life, and no one loses these needs.

There is a need to look toward different roles, for both the middle-aged and aged, ones that are grounded on concepts of shared responsibility and equality of power and control. In order to do this, the need sometimes arises to forego our earlier relationships with our parents.

Regardless of how much you got (or didn't get) from your parents, it is possible for relationships to change. The change, however, should not be that of parenting your parents; it is time now to consider a new and different kind of relationship, one of adult child to your parents.

The Future – Filial Maturity:

> *You honor your parents most by growing up yourself.* – Ben Weininger

Our society has barely begun to cope with the physical, emotional, financial and social problems elderly people present for the middle-aged generation and for society. The traditional definitions of an adult's responsibilities toward aging parents are now largely outmoded or inadequate. This middle generation is expected to create a fresh set of personal standards and ways of dealing with aging parents.

Adult children have an important task, referred to as filial maturity, that involves transforming their relationship with their parents. Adults must learn to relate to their parents as adults, not as children or as parents. They need to consider and meet their own needs, set limits while at the same time giving their parents the kind of help they need without feeling overwhelmed. You will know when you have achieved filial maturity when you can forgive your parents, recognize their real needs, say to yourself "my parents did the best job they could," and accept them as adult human beings. If adult children feel forgotten and unappreciated, as they often do, it will be difficult for them to establish new purposes, alter their commitments and learn new ways of making this new relationship with their parents work. These are qualities that an adult child and their elderly relative can strive towards. *A new and better relationship with your elderly parent is a gift of friendship not a duty or obligation.*

If love, compassion and caring are what you are really trying to demonstrate, then you need to use a language that communicates what you really want to say, one that helps to unravel and discover who your parents or elderly relative really are. It's easy to busy ourselves with a variety of tasks and activities. Much more important is talking and acting out the language of love. Changing our attitude towards an aging relative – parent, spouse or sibling – is a very difficult task. That is what filial maturity is all about. Who you are and what you want are important questions to ask yourself. What are your rights and needs? Adult children struggle to understand and cope with aging parents. Often these relationships are dominated by concern and compassion leading to feelings of obligation or duty that often continue for a long time. Possibly the point at which adult children achieve filial maturity is the point at which they assume responsibility for some aspects of their parents' lives and live with the results of those decisions.

Not all relationships between parents and their children are characterized by these close emotional ties. Spending time with a relative you don't like can be a most difficult situation to overcome. Many people just give up and withdraw from their elderly relative for very good reasons.

This above all: to thine own self be true,
And it must follow, as the night the day,
Thou canst not then be false to any man.
– Hamlet

As in any relationship, the extent of your happiness is based on how you feel about yourself. How you really feel about yourself began to develop when you were an infant. Now, as an adult, you may find that assuming responsibility for an aging parent is overwhelming because you carry so much excess baggage from the past. If you are still seeking your parents approval and love (which many of us are doing consciously or unconsciously) you may never come close to enjoying any time together.

Just plain *talking* about your elderly relatives with friends helps to get things off your chest and lessen the burden that you may be carrying. That's what letting go is all about. When talking about how you feel doesn't help, try *doing* something in a different way. Take a good look at what you're doing now and make one tiny change. That's right, just one. If changing a habit doesn't work, it might be time to seek professional help.

It is fair to say that future generations of old people will be different. They will be better educated, have more money, have higher expectations of quality and quantity of services. And although we think we know what society's goals should be – giving emotional support to older people, helping to motivate and activate them, avoiding relocation and bringing services to them rather than bringing the elderly to the service – here are some additional considerations. One of the most pleasant thoughts for any human being is that they are needed, that they are important enough and competent enough to help and to add to the happiness of other people. How can we include old people in our society, how can we give them the sense of purpose they spent a lifetime trying to find, how can we help them meet their emotional needs as well as physical needs? This is our challenge.

The Art of Maturity

The distilled experience of many men has resulted in discoveries like these about the art of mature living . . . That life is too short to be wasted in hatred, revenge, fault-finding, prejudice, intolerance and destruction. That moderation in all things is a good rule. It is wise to live a balanced and varied life without permitting anyone or anything to enslave us. That we must learn to distinguish between the important and unimportant. Then trifles will not trip us up and we can devote our lives to the meaningful and the significant. – Author Unknown

3
Nursing Homes

With the redefinition and extension of old age within this century, we are simply unprepared for this final, lengthy stage of life. We have no previous path to follow when it comes to the question of institutionalizing our loved ones. Should my spouse or parent be institutionalized? We complicate matters further by asking: What will people think if I put my elderly relative in an institution? For spouse or adult child, these are real difficulties.

The challenge, then, is to re-examine our values and beliefs, to look at our lives from a slight distance, to feel that we are doing (and will do) the best we can for our elderly relative. This does not mean a total abdication of our own lives. It means finding a balance for ourselves with practical help, emotional and/or financial support, and continued involvement in the life of our elderly relative.

When one member's abilities begin to diminish noticeably, the usual ways of being, interacting and doing things within the family begin to change. This change sifts down throughout the family as various members begin to take over certain responsibilities or to abdicate others. When parents or spouse become disabled in any way, it often alters the relationships of the other family members. For the caregiver this can involve feelings of generally being "out of sync" with oneself and with relatives, or feelings of anger and rage as some other members of the family move to the back seat, a position from which no useful steering can occur.

Decisions have to be made. Many difficulties must be resolved for the benefit of the elderly person. One of the major decisions is a move to an institution. Facing this decision can invoke a myriad of other major issues as well as overwhelming feelings and doubts: Am I doing the right thing? Should I move my mother whether she thinks she needs daily care or not? Should she move in with me, after all she looked after me all those years of growing up? She won't know anyone in a care facility. She'll have to give up all of her familiar surroundings, friends in the "block," community stores and possessions. How will she be treated? Shouldn't I be doing more and more?

Many people ask these questions and would give anything to be able to prolong their relative's independent years in the hope that they will never have to face these issues. Feelings of anger, resentment, sadness and fear are natural when you have to watch your elderly relative move from independence to dependency. Before making any decisions, you will want to first consider the alternatives to institutional care.

ALTERNATIVES TO INSTITUTIONAL CARE

Services Available in the Community: Services for the elderly differ greatly from one location to another. Also, many of the same services come under different names. The following information from British Columbia, Canada, is included here to give you an idea of their diversity. Variations may be available in your area and costs will vary. Some of these services may be partly paid for by medical plans. Information may be found at local health units, community centers and recreation centers, the public library and, in the United States, at the local Area Agency on Aging offices. Your family doctor may be able to tell you about services available in your area:

Home Care Service: At-home professional care by doctors, nurses and in some areas by physiotherapists, occupational or speech therapists, nutritionists or social workers.

Homemaker Services: Help with daily tasks like laundry, housework, and bathing, grooming and shopping.

Assistance in Modifying Your Home: Personnel at a health unit, family doctor or occupational therapist can advise you about helpful modifications.

Volunteer Services: One-to-one visiting, shopping, readers for partially sighted or blind, telephone check, information and friendship.

Meals on Wheels: Meals delivered by volunteers to the homes of health impaired people who are unable to adequately provide themselves with food.

Wheels to Meals: Transportation provided to centers serving meals.

Transportation Services: A door-to-door service for people who cannot use regular buses.

Adult Day Care: Adult day care centers provide supervised activities, monitoring of health needs, hot meals, opportunities for social and recreational programs and sometimes transportation to and from the center.

The following provide respite, as one aspect of their services, for caregiving families while their health impaired relative is receiving day care:

Day Hospital: Similar to adult day care centers but provides more medical and rehabilitation services.

Respite Care/Short Stay Beds: Short Stay hospital beds are a back-up service to whatever home care you provide. These beds provide relief of care to family members who become ill or go on holiday. They are located in some of the care facilities and must be pre-booked for vacation times.

Schools of Nursing: Student nurses may be hired to provide help.

Short Stay Assessment and Treatment Centers: Hospital centers for those whose needs go beyond assessment and treatment available in the community (available for in and out patients). Referral from a physician or community health worker is necessary.

Health-related services available in many North American communities include the following (the titles of these services or groups may be different in your area):

Alcohol and Drug Programs
Alzheimer's Society or Support Groups
Arthritis Society
Heart and Stroke Association and Clubs
Parkinson's Disease Association
Huntington's Society
Cancer Society
Diabetes Association
Institute for the Blind
Institute for the Deaf
Paraplegic Association
St. John's Ambulance
Red Cross
Medic-Alert
Ostop Society

Ostomy Association
Association of Naturopathic Physicians
Holistic Healing Association
Counselling Agencies
- Secular organizations
- Religious Organizations

Legal Advice
- Lawyer Referral Service
- Public Legal Education Society
- Dial-a-law
- Legal Assistance Society

Ask your doctor, or local health unit about a specific group or health condition if it is not listed here.

WHEN TO CONSIDER ENTERING A NURSING HOME

> *Give us serenity to accept what cannot be changed; courage to change what should be changed, and wisdom to distinguish the one from the other.* – Reinhold Niebuhr

One of the saddest duties in life is making a decision to institutionalize an elderly parent or spouse. Although many families would prefer that their elderly relatives live with them, there are circumstances in which institutional care becomes necessary. The thought of removing our elderly loved ones from most of their possessions, the familiar spaces and places that are a large part of their identity, is painful. This will be, in nearly all cases, a final move. The heartfelt cry, "How could I do this to my father, he cared for me and now I have put him in a prison where he will die," is a common one. The emotional impact of this decision is very strong. When this happens, adult children or an elderly spouse should not view this as a sign of failure. Nor should they see it as an opportunity to give up all interest and responsibility.

Hard Choices: The decision to relocate an elderly relative is one some of you have already experienced; some of you are at the point of knowing that a decision to relocate is imminent. Many of you will find yourselves in a state of crisis even if you have been working at and discussing plans to change the living situation. Those of you who think you are years away from this decision may be right; but you are wise to make some plans now. Emergency situations have a way of forcing decisions or of making them for us. You may be one of the lucky ones who will never have to make this decision: your aging parent or spouse will finish his/her time at home.

Family caregivers make decisions when under great emotional strain from the task of looking after an elderly person. Families provide the majority of care to their elderly members for as long as possible. Wise decisions cannot be made when the demands become too great: for example, the health of the elderly person deteriorates, or the caregiver's situation alters (she may take a full time job, be forced to move, or become ill or exhausted and need a change). The topic of living accommodation is often ignored. It is crucial that you discuss this important issue with elderly relatives before a crisis.

Who Decides: If at all possible, older people should be involved in the decision to move. Some make this decision on their own. They may admit that meals are becoming too difficult to prepare, they are afraid of falling or staying alone. Perhaps there is no one else to look after their needs. At other times, an objective health professional called in by a neighbor, friend or relative will make the decision. Most often, however, it is a family member who must take decisive action.

One way to start is with an open and frank discussion of the elderly person's situation and yours. In this way you can start planning for a change before a crisis. Living with the consequences of emotional decisions can be more stressful than the situation that precipitated a crisis.

So sad, so strange, the days that are no more. – Alfred Tennyson

Along with old age can come the loss of spouse and friends. Ability to shop and to cook diminish. Possible memory loss and chronic illnesses may begin to accumulate making living alone increasingly difficult. The elderly person may simply not wish to confront the realities of the ongoing and increasing need for continual care. When the subject is broached you may get a reaction like "over my dead body am I going to live in a Nursing Home." Unfortunately, it's most often your body that's going to suffer. An elderly relative may also snap, "Not you or anyone else is going to put me in a Home." In some instances, families will have to allow elderly relatives to stay in their own home or apartment as long as they are not a danger to others. Families may need to "live with" and respect the rights of the elderly person even under the most undesirable and devastating of situations.

When the amount of care needed or demanded by the elderly person becomes too much of a strain on the main caregiver, a move to a care facility is necessary. When an elderly person does not want to move, vacillates between moving and not moving, or is in too unhealthy a state to make a decision, then the decision may have to be made for them. Some elderly people think they are managing perfectly well on their own because they are unaware of the numerous "props" and supports that help keep them in their own home or apartment. If possible, you may have to gently (or firmly) point out all the things that are being done by you or by others. This may help the older person realize the situation.

Not many of us can remove the "props" and watch our elderly relatives struggle. It is simply too difficult for us to stand by and observe their decline. This may be the time to rely on professionals. They may have to step in and "make" a move happen. A hard line, perhaps, but better a hard line than having an elderly person and caregiver hanging on to the end of a rope.

Discussions centering on relocating an elderly relative are not always easy. If approached with a caring attitude this topic can be talked about from time to time, so that the possibility of surprises or an emergency will be easier to handle. If possible, discussions should include other members of the family and the doctor. Any decisions that are agreed to will have been shared and made over the course of time, with the best interests of everyone given due consideration.

Now could be a good time to arrange talking with your parents or spouse. You may want to write down a few scenarios that could be titled "What happens if..." and take them with you. Here are a few to get you started:

- What happens if . . . one of you died tomorrow, would you want to continue living in this big home or apartment by yourself?
- What happens if . . . you had a stroke and could not manage living alone?
- What happens if . . . your friend Alice can no longer take you shopping and to the bank?

Often you must make the decision to move your elderly relative into an institution. No one can fully appreciate the difficulty of such a decision unless they have had a similar experience. So don't expect people to understand. It takes courage to face issues, the problems which, if not acted upon, can remain unresolved indefinitely. It also takes courage to risk a wrong decision, as it is often easier to make no decision at all. Ask yourself:

- How will my life be different after I've made this decision (in practical terms)?

- How much will my parent gain? lose? in the move?
- How much will I gain? lose? in the move?
- How will I feel?
- Have I tried all the available resources and options?
- Have I done my best?

When you have to make a choice and don't make it, that in itself is a choice. – W. James

It is important to recognize that some older people manage quite well in institutions. A few do even better, and enjoy it more, than living alone without friends or relatives to assist in daily living. We can try to maintain our elderly relatives in their own homes for as long as possible. But not at all costs, financial or emotional, to family members.

When making decisions about the need for institutionalization careful attention should be paid to guilt feelings. Family members who allow guilt to fester may discontinue their involvement, after the elderly person has entered a care facility. Others sacrifice their personal lives for the remaining years of their institutionalized relative's life. Surely there is a middle road.

One of the most important things to recognize and remember is this: step back, not just a step or two, but at least a dozen. What type of life and living do your parents have now? How would it be different if they were in an institution? You may not be making a drastic change in their quality of life. So often, when this relocation decision must be made, we think of our parents as they once were – vital, strong, supportive – instead of how they are now, becoming more dependent, possibly frail, in need of daily care. Once we accept the latter, more realistic view, a move to institution life may not seem as drastic. It is a fact of life, for the present, that institutions are necessary for a proportion of our elderly. When we discover a better solution we'll let you know.

GUIDELINES FOR CONSIDERING A MOVE

Now that you have given careful thought to the decision to relocate a parent or spouse, these guidelines will help you further explore the possible necessity for a move. These are not hard and fast rules; rather they are a guide. If many factors on these lists are present you will have a good indication that a move may be necessary.

Caregiver:

1. you "burn out" or become ill
2. you change employment status (take a full-time or part-time job out of the home)
3. your family responsibilities and social life are suffering
4. your elderly relative needs an ever-increasing amount of time
5. your friends have been cut off because of demands of caring for your elderly relative
6. you've been accused of stealing money or poisoning food
7. neighbors have been pressuring you because they are being "bothered" by your relative

Resident:

Personal needs

1. needs help to use the bathroom, bathe, dress, shave
2. is unable to launder clothing and bedding when necessary
3. mixes up day and night, does their laundry at 4:00 a.m.
4. shows disinterest in grooming or using cosmetics

Safety

1. may be a danger to themselves or others: when smoking they leave a lit cigarette in the ashtray or miss the ashtray with their ashes
2. accidents: falling, increased car accidents
3. gets lost in familiar situations
4. may wander away
5. a home or apartment needs major modifications

Medical

1. has had a recent discharge from hospital
2. has multiple medical problems
3. has physical immobility or other physical handicaps
4. has incontinence
5. is mentally impaired
6. is losing daily living skills
7. doesn't sleep well and therefore disturbs others at night
8. forgets to take medications or takes them inappropriately
9. is unable to get help if needed

Social:

1. is living alone due to death, divorce or separation

2. has no nearby relatives
3. lives in social isolation
4. exhibits inappropriate behavior: exposing themselves, dressing inappropriately for the weather
5. develops aggression and agitation, explosiveness, depression, apathy, paranoia, disorientation: does not know who the family is

Nutritional

1. shopping becomes too difficult
2. getting meals becomes too difficult
3. needing help to eat or forgetting to eat at all
4. weight loss

Other Considerations

1. inability to handle money
2. expressing a desire to die

It is vital that you keep part of life for yourself, otherwise you will "burn out." When you have done all you can do for your elderly relative (including exhausting the community services), then it is time to consider a care facility. Institutions are your next option for caring for physically and/or mentally impaired persons who have reached the stage of needing more help than their families can manage. An institution can provide supervision, personal assistance, sound nutrition, recreational activities and skilled nursing care on a 24-hour basis.

SELECTING A NURSING HOME

Where To Go For Help: Once the decision is made, you will need to get sound advice about the care facilities in your region. Here's where you can start:

1. Ask friends and relatives who either work in the field or who have been through the experience; or friends may be able to refer you to someone who has.
2. Discuss the situation with your doctor and your relative's doctor; two points of view are often helpful. The doctor may or may not be familiar with the Nursing Home situation in your area but should be able to refer you to the appropriate place.
3. Call your local health unit or public health authority (in the government pages of the phone book). Be prepared to make a lot of phone calls.

4. Hospital Social Service Departments may be able to give you information on their services and those in the surrounding area.
5. You may want to contact your local seniors' center, disabled association, old age pensioners' group or veterans' association for information.

Types and Level of Care: There are vast differences in types and level of care facilities across North America. The whole topic of care facilities is quite overwhelming even to some seasoned professionals who work in the field. In fact, the variety of names alone is enough to throw anyone into a tail spin:

Homes for the Aged
Guest Homes
Care Homes
Lodges
Adult Foster Care
Long Term Care Facility
Intermediate Care Facility
Skilled Nursing Facility
Chronic Care
Palliative/Hospice Care
Rest Homes
Nursing Homes
Institution
Boarding Homes
Auxiliary Hospitals
Personal Care Facility
Extended Care Facility
Old Folks Homes
Residential Care
Sheltered Housing

Is it any wonder that the average Joe or Joan may get confused? Not included in this list are such places as retirement villages and communities, as many of them do not offer medical care. Care facilities or institutions for the elderly may be government- owned, charitable institutions or privately-owned.

Level of Care: Health systems, facilities and terms vary from region to region throughout Canada and the U.S.A. In general, "Nursing Homes" range from offering minimal help with daily activities, personal care, social and recreational activities to offering 24-hour professional nursing care. Nursing Homes are for those who are physically and/or mentally handicapped, who have difficulty coping with the daily tasks of living, who need more assistance and care (professional or otherwise) than family members can give, and who need more resources than those available in-home or from the community.

In some areas an assessor from the Health Department will determine the level of care required, in other areas a doctor will make a medical evaluation. They will tell you which facilities provide the kind of care you need and information about waiting lists. Finding out what level of care your elderly relative needs is one way to narrow your options of care facilities. In other locations you will need to visit many Nursing Homes to find out what type of home will best suit your parents' needs and lifestyle.

Financial Resources: Methods of financing and financial resources may be the determining factor in the decision to institutionalize your elderly relative, and in the choice of Nursing Homes. This will vary from state to state and province to province. You will need to determine your financial situation and personal resources. Families must also consider the mental and emotional well-being of their members. This "cost" must be weighed against the financial expense of living in an institution. Be sure to understand clearly how the various financial policies and programs will pay for Nursing Home care.

In the United States, for instance, private insurance policies do not necessarily cover Nursing Home benefits. Medicare payments are also limited to specific circumstances and are not intended for long-term nursing care. Medicaid is available for people who need nursing home care and who qualify because of low income. If, however, your relative enters a Nursing Home as a "private- pay" resident and funds become depleted it is important to have selected a nursing home that participates in the Medicaid program; this will allow them to remain in the same home.

In Canada, "private-pay" residents who seek accommodation in privately-operated facilities are not always given financial assistance. Many other Nursing Homes are subsidized. Here is an example of one Canadian subsidized system, British Columbia Long Term Care Program.[1]

Daily Charge

The total daily charge is made up of:

(a) Your portion of daily charge (the user charge) which represents approximately 75% of Old Age Security and guaranteed Income Supplement cheques. This amount will increase with any increases in these two pension cheques.

(b) The Long Term Care portion funded by the Ministry of Health. This payment is made directly to the facility by the Provincial Government.

The total payment provides you with accommodation, laundry, professional supervision as necessary to the level of care provided, a program of social functions, entertainment and recreational activities.

Allowable Extra Charges

In some facilities, a differential payment has been approved by Long Term Care for single or double rooms of superior quality.

Extra charges will be made for: personal hygiene supplies purchased on your behalf (e.g., toothpaste, deodorant, denture cleanser, talcum powder, cosmetics, nail polish, soap of personal preference, etc.); cablevision for use in your room; personal telephone; newspapers; dry cleaning; repairs to electrical razors and other personal equipment.

You will also be required to purchase any special equipment for your own use (e.g., wheelchairs, walkers, and special medication which is not paid for by Pharmacare).

Time Spent Away From The Facility

You may make a request to spend some time away from the facility each year. If your request is approved, you will be expected to continue to pay the user charge during your absence and the Long Term Care portion of payment will be continued.

Hospitalization

Your portion of the daily charge at the facility must be paid, even if you are hospitalized.

Guaranteed Income Supplement (G.I.S.)

Eligibility for Guaranteed Income Supplement is solely related to income, and does not cease when client is admitted to a facility. Application must be made each year.

The Provincial Guaranteed Available Income for Need Cheque (G.A.I.N.)

Is discontinued on admission to a facility.

Handicapped Persons Income Assistance (H.P.I.A.)

Is discontinued on admission to a facility, but Ministry of Human Resources will pay daily charge, a clothing allowance and a monthly comfort allowance.

Old Age Pension

A married couple may apply for two single persons' pension allowance when one is placed in a facility and the other is still living at home.

[Selecting a care facility takes time and careful planning. After you have narrowed down your options by considering level and type of care and financial resources you may have two or more facilities that fit your criteria. It may be difficult to find the perfect fit. It is best to visit at least three facilities, even if your relative never needs to go to a Nursing Home. If possible take your relative with you so that you can discuss the home, its advantages and disadvantages to both of you. For instance, proximity to your own home will make visiting easier.

Give careful consideration to selecting a care facility that fits the personal characteristics of your relative. For instance, is there a sewing room available to your mother who has always enjoyed making things? Four star Nursing Homes do not necessarily ensure top quality attitude and care. It's not watering the plants that counts, it's nurturing the people.

When you visit a care facility, keep your eyes and ears well open for important yet subtle or hidden qualities. For example, locate the activity room and check it at different times of the day; is anyone using it? Take the Facility Tour Checklist with you. Make notes on your tour just as you would if you were visiting houses for sale.]

There is more to a long-term-care facility than a safe and comfortable environment. The attitude of the administrator and the care staff is important to the residents, and the facility should be operated in a manner that will respect and maintain the spirit, dignity and individuality of each resident.

Schedule an appointment to visit, talk with the person in charge and view the facility. Plan to spend sufficient time at the facility; a hasty tour will not help you make the best decision. Please respect the privacy of the residents as you make your tour.

Don't be afraid to ask questions and use the following information as a guide. Read through the list and make a note of the things you and your relative would really like or dislike, keeping in mind that it is unlikely that any one facility will be able to fulfill all your needs and expectations. [(Ask for the Nursing Home brochure that includes information on their policies, costs, medical coverage, what you can bring, services, social and recreational activities, and transportation.)]

FACILITY TOUR CHECKLIST

As you tour the facility, observe the following:

The conditions of the building, the grounds, and attitude of staff:

Are they pleasant, friendly and cheerful?
How do they address the residents?
Do they answer requests promptly and courteously?
Do they respect residents' privacy (knocking on doors before entering, etc.)?
Do residents appear sociable and at home with their surroundings?
Is the home clean and free from offensive odor?
Is there a lounge for socializing and entertaining visitors? Is it used?
Is there space for private conversations with family and friends?
Is there an area or special room for crafts and other activities (movies, entertainment, etc.)?
Is there a garden or patio? Can the residents go outside?
Is there a ramp for wheelchairs?

Residents' Rooms

Observe:

The general appearance and size.
Is there good window area? What does the window look out upon?
Is the bed comfortable?
Is there a comfortable chair?
How much storage space?
Is there a locked cupboard or drawer?
Do the residents have their own possessions and furniture in their rooms indicating their individuality?
Is it possible to have your own telephone and television?

Ask:

How close is the bathroom? Is it shared or private?
Is there a call bell or call light system, or an intercom for calling care staff?

Are you able to lock your door if you wish?

May you hang your own pictures and bring some of your own furniture?

What provision has been made for couples who wish to share a room?

May you get up in the morning when you wish?

May you stay up at night as long as you desire?

May you choose your roommate?

May you move to another room if you wish?

Are private rooms available? Is there an extra charge?

Food Service

Observe:

Is there a separate dining room? What type of meal service? Cafeteria style, etc.?

How far is it from the residents' rooms to the dining room?

Where do residents eat their meals if there is no dining room?

Are residents allowed enough time to eat meals at their own pace?

Is there more than one sitting?

Are menus posted?

Does the meal match the posted menu?

Ask:

May you choose where you will sit in the dining room?

Is room service available?

What are the meal times? Are they flexible?

Are special diets available?

Are there snacks available between meals?

Is there help available for residents who are unable to cut up their own food or feed themselves?

Can the resident or relative make a cup of tea or coffee when they wish?

May residents have guests to a meal? How much will this cost? How much notice is required?

Policies

Find out about the policies of the home:

Will you be encouraged to participate with staff in identification of your own care requirements?

Who is responsible for transporting you to medical offices or other outside appointments?

What is the procedure for identifying personal items (e.g., clothing, furniture, dentures, eyeglasses, etc.) and what is the policy regarding lost articles?

What are the smoking regulations?

When are the fire drills and what are the procedures?

Is food or alcohol permitted in your room?

What are the policies regarding money and valuables?

Is there a residents' council to handle specific concerns of the residents within the facility?

Physician:

Can your own doctor continue to care for you in this facility?

How often do doctors visit?

Pharmacy Services:

What arrangements does the facility have for pharmacy services?

May you get your own prescription filled?

May you keep non-prescription medicines at your bedside?

Who is responsible for administering medication?

Can you approve purchases made on your behalf prior to purchase? Are the bills itemized (e.g., personal grooming supplies and medication not covered by Pharmacare)?

Laundry:

What items of personal clothing may be sent to the laundry?

May you do your own personal laundry?

What laundry facilities are available for residents' use?

Who is responsible for mending of personal clothing?

Resident Care:

Are visitors welcome at any time?
How much professional help is available (social worker, dietician, rehabilitation therapist, doctor, registered or graduate nurses, clergy)?
Who is the Director of Resident Care?
What services will the care staff provide?
Are hairdressing and barber services available?
Does a podiatrist visit?
Who is on duty at night?
If staff do not wear uniforms, how do you identify them?
Who should be contacted if you have a question regarding your rights or the services available?

Bathing:

May you have a bath when and as often as you wish?
May you use your own soap and shampoo, etc.?
Will you have privacy for your bath?
May you have a shower if you prefer?

Social and Recreational Activities:

What kind of organized activities are there available?
Are all the entertainment and activity functions in-house, or are outside facilities utilized, e.g. community centres, theatres, etc.?
Is there a variety of craft activities?
Are there extra charges for craft materials?
Will you be able to pursue your own hobbies? (gardening, cooking, playing a musical instrument, billiards, bowling, swimming, etc.)
Do the residents appear to come and go as they please?
Is there a signing-out book?
Is there a telephone available to all residents which is private and easy to reach?
Is your language spoken? If not, how will the staff communicate with you?
Are church services held in the facility?
Are volunteers active in the facility?

[Reprinted with kind permission from the City of Vancouver Health Department.]

ADJUSTING TO LIVING IN A NURSING HOME

If I were only
A child again
No one's ever been so
Good to me since then
Everywhere I looked it
Seemed so colour bright.
–Curtis Mayfield

Prolonged living requires aging people to make an unusual number of adjustments. This is especially so when they enter a Nursing Home. Often elderly residents do not feel useful or needed and really have little or no purpose for living in a society that has emphasized independence and productivity. There is little space for cherished possessions, for some people the only things that maintain a sense of who they are. This loss of self-identity can manifest itself in a withdrawal from the activities of daily living and the downward spiral of deteriorating health may begin.

To give you some ideas of the losses consider the following scenario:

Have you ever tried packing all of your possessions into two suitcases, even for a weekend holiday? What do I need if it rains, but it's supposed to be sunny? I think I'll take my favorite pillow, too; I never seem to get a good night's sleep without it. And so it goes, all those decisions, and that's just for a two day get-away.

And how about part of your identity, all the "things" you have around you? What possessions do you really cherish, how important are they to you, what would you miss most if your house burned down? Go ahead right now, look around your place, what would you really want to have with you and what couldn't you do without if you had to pack it into two suitcases?

The decisions may be so difficult that you would decide to take nothing. But whether you take a few things or none at all, you will leave behind a part of you, part of your self and therefore part of your identity. I recently had friends staying with me in my one bedroom apartment. After a couple of days of looking around and naturally touching everything, the little five year old said to me, "Wendy, your apartment looks like a music store." How could I cram my musical collection into two suitcases? I cannot imagine.

You can be of great help and support to your relative at this time. Material possessions often represent a person's lifetime. Because of limited space in a nursing home, items to be taken there must to be selected with great care. Many nursing homes do not accommodate large pieces of furniture. Sometimes there is room for a favorite chair, and smaller things like pictures, a clock, radio, TV, plants, or books can be taken. In some instances you will have to do the selecting without your relative. This can be a lonely and difficult task: good friends can help you with this painful process. Even without large items of furniture you can help make a small space into a homey place for your elderly relative. These possessions bring continuity with the past and can help reduce the stress of institutional living.

Helping Your Relative Adjust: Entering a care facility is a very stressful experience for most people. This change in living situation creates major adjustments for the elderly person. It is therefore a time when staff, residents and members must work together to ease what can be a very painful time. Two important things to remember at this difficult time of adjustment are:

1. maintain family relationships; be involved with the elderly member of your family;

2. keep the lines of communication open with your elderly relative, with staff, and friends.

Choice/Control: Elderly people need time to adjust. While not always a completely negative experience, living in a care facility means a loss of control over many aspects of life. Loss of health, physical, mental or in some instances both. Loss of economic status including worry about financial matters (e.g., how long will my life savings last?) Loss of home, neighbors, a pet. These losses can be cause for depression, anger, frustration or reduced self-esteem.

Along with institutional life comes the loss of personal freedoms and adjustment to routines such as: meal times, menus, noisy dining rooms, rising and bed times, recreation schedules, rotating staff, lack of privacy, limited physical and personal space. In some Nursing Homes residents must contend with disrespectful or belittling staff attitudes.

The right to choices and the opportunity to make decisions are important human qualities. When we lose our right to choose we become depersonalized and dependent. Some residents will "act out" like children often do. To maintain or regain control over their lives, they may withdraw from life or even become suicidal. Control, choices and opportunities for making decisions are extremely important to elderly persons. Following are some ways giving the elderly some control over part of their life in institutions.

1. a bedtime that can be flexible;
2. flexibility over meal time or menu selection;
3. allowing the resident to choose how he/she would like to be addressed;
4. knocking and asking permission before entering her/his room;
5. going for an outing or staying home;
6. type of plants he/she would like;
7. deciding what clothes to wear each day;
8. deciding who he/she would like to have visit;
9. decorating her/his own room;
10. giving to others.

Residents in many instances, must learn to live with at least one roommate, in some cases two or three. When to visit, when to open windows or draw curtains, where to put furniture, when to use the bathroom, radio, lights, all need to be considered. Another major area of adjustment is that of personal hygiene. How would you feel being bathed and toileted by someone else?

To know how to grow old is the
master-work of wisdom, and one of
the most difficult chapters in the great
art of living.
–Henri Frederic Amiel

TAKING CARE OF YOURSELF

After your elderly relative enters a nursing home you may also experience a period of adjustment. Many family members, particularly those who are the main visitor, may find little relief after the move has been made. In fact, in many cases visiting family members carry as much of a load after an elderly relative moves into a care facility as before they moved. The stresses of daily or weekly visiting and feelings about no longer being able to care for the elderly person at home, and perhaps some feelings of guilt are difficult to come to terms with.

CHECKLIST FOR TAKING CARE OF YOURSELF

- Group discussion and support groups are helpful in resolving feelings of guilt, anger and resentment. Sharing experiences, ventilating feelings and defining your role and that of the nursing home staff are important.
- Through educational programs, a knowledge of the mental and physical aspects of aging can help to alleviate some of the stresses.
- Utilizing relief programs for family visitors (for instance, more extensive use of volunteer visitors) paid companions and respite care could ease the burden. Ask for professional and/or volunteer help.
- You don't need to defend yourself to your family members or friends after your elderly relative has entered a care facility. You and/or your relative have made the decision based on many aspects of the situation that others have little knowledge of, unless of course they were involved in the decision.
- It will be important for you to set limits: a reasonable amount of time and energy for your relative's care and a reasonable amount of time and energy for yourself (spending some time doing things that for you are fun, spending time with friends).
- Plan and take a regular break from visiting your elderly relative.
- Ask other family members to share the responsibility or ask a doctor, clergy or friend to ask your family for help.
- Familiarize yourself with all the available community resources and use them.
- When someone offers to help you, give them something specific to do.
- If you are withdrawing from others and have no laughter and enjoyment in life, talk to your friends or see a professional.
- If your friends or other people suggest that you might benefit from talking to a professional, they may be right.
- Take care of your own health.

CULTURAL DIFFERENCES

Hanukkah, kosher food, Chinese New Year and Christmas, all under the same roof. Most Nursing Homes accommodate residents from a wide variety of ethnic backgrounds. These cultural differences involve such things as language, food, religion, customs, dress and music. Some facilities accommodate a specific ethnic group and provide an environment including staff who speak the language, provide food or music that allows for continuity of one's own culture. Other care facilities allow for these cultural differences by celebrating special events, ethnic holidays and musical programs.

In some instances language barriers do exist between residents and between residents and staff. Some facilities have language banks, a list of staff members or individuals who can speak other languages. They can be called upon when the need arises, for example, to translate a letter. Ask the administrator of the facility about volunteers from other countries, clergy who speak your relative's language, reading material including newspapers and library books in languages other than English.

Some people carry prejudices toward other groups from their childhood. Elderly residents may be adamant against being given care by a staff member of different ethnic origin or different sex. There are no easy solutions when these difficulties exist. You may need to discuss, in advance, with your elderly relative that nursing homes employ people from many different backgrounds. Allowing your relative to express feelings and talk about it with you may lead to some acceptance of this sensitive situation.

CHANGING FACILITIES

The time may come when your elderly relative can no longer remain in the Home. For a variety of reasons, including inadequate fire safety, poor nutritional standards, impersonal atmosphere, or negative attitude, you may be forced to change facilities. If your attempts to solve the problems with appropriate people (resident, person in charge of resident care, administrator, or owner) have not been successful, your options involve getting a list of nursing homes in your area from the public health unit or library. Talk to clergy or members of various support groups. They may have a friend or relative in a nursing home and may be able to recommend a good one.

4
Portraits of Visiting

Visiting is for some a business-like task or a duty that is seldom enjoyed. For others it is a tormenting nightmare. But visiting can also be a satisfying and rewarding part of your day or week. "Quality" visiting implies the pursuit of excellence or even a striving for perfection. The word "quality" is used to conjure up a picture of satisfaction, of meaningfulness, ultimately of reciprocal enjoyment.

This chapter describes the visiting process from two perspectives: that of the visiting relative and that of the elderly resident. The following portraits illustrate individual differences and interactions occurring between residents and their relatives during actual visiting time. They emphasize the importance of feelings and relationships. Details are selected to depict the realities of visiting. Naturally, not all visitors experience all of these issues and problems. Some deal with them better than others and, for a variety of reasons, others acknowledge few concerns. These portraits describe some widely acknowledged components of the visiting process – a process that began many years before the institutionalization of your relative.

THE ENVIRONMENT

It all began six years ago when the construction was completed. The empty lot had been a real "dumping ground." Dumping elderly relatives in nursing homes is a common myth in our society today. (In fact, families do not "dump" their elderly relatives in a nursing home, nor do they abandon them after placement.) When the dirt and stumps were cleared away, what appeared was an attractive and carefully constructed long-term care facility. One by one, family members carefully helped their loved ones into their rooms. And with much sadness, often with feelings of guilt, they drove away to their own homes. At least, this is how it was for most. Now they would begin to experience a newly-created, ill-explored role in life, that of visitor to an institutionalized elderly relative.

It just happened to be a glorious day – a rare occasion in this west coast Canadian city. Folks think they're lucky when they get one of these "Vancouver specials" during the winter months. Beads of moisture hung on the trees and bushes. As I drove down the crescent I passed a large shopping mall, a perfectly nestled little park, and a neighborhood pub within a small shopping center. An elderly gentleman sat waiting for the bus. Then the large clear sign, The Royal Way Care Home, appeared.

Its location had been well thought out. The circular drive made for easy pick up and drop off. Stalls for visitor parking were conveniently located close to the front door (wheel chair accessible, of course). A Royal Way van was stationed at the front door. As I headed toward the white brick structure surrounded by lovely shrubs and flat crackless pavement, a well manicured lawn saying "keep off" made me wonder about my welcome. The area surrounding the building seemed to be very well planned – walkways to the back were surrounded by foliage and a wild section of forest had been left creating a quiet environment for nature lovers. One could wander outdoors in a wheelchair or walker and even hear the birds. A high wire fence around the outside of the property aroused my curiosity. Was the inside as secure and safe? At what price? Nonetheless, the setting was magnificent. On the outside, the facility was elaborately constructed to meet every special need.

As I approached the front door I passed a lady, bucket and window washer in hand. She greeted me with a friendly hello. Right inside the door sat two elderly gentlemen, one with his walker beside him, the other with a cane. I said, "good morning," and they both smiled. The receptionist looked up from her typewriter and I introduced myself. She had been expecting me. Everyone and everything was welcoming.

The little store off the foyer was open for business, equipped with the usual necessities, toothpaste and candies, and was staffed by a woman of 85 years. A fine looking woman, well-wrinkled with thinning hair, Dorothy, announced, "I haven't seen you before. You'll have to speak loudly as I'm a bit deaf, so I usually do most of the talking. It's easier that way." She was visiting with another resident who had come down for her morning wheelchair cruise. I made a purchase and moved on into the foyer.

In a convenient, cozy meeting place a few residents were watching the morning news on TV. A motorized wheelchair maneuvered between the high-seated arm-chairs and the driver spoke of his newly-acquired skill. The activity director's office was directly opposite this hub of activity, her door wide open. Sally was a friend to all and my tour of the facility was heightened by her extraordinary personality. Not only did she co-ordinate all of the residents' activities, she was counsellor, problem solver, challenger, motivator, stimulator – you name it. The warmth and friendliness which seemed everywhere impressed me.

The hallways were wide, and large windows opened onto a patio. Benches were placed everywhere. There was a residents' kitchen, hairdresser and barber shop, a small laundromat, volunteer office and a meeting room where residents could still be part of decisions in their Home. The walls were decorated with some residents' artwork from arts and crafts activities, a homey touch. We passed a well-stocked library, a games and exercise room and a current events board which read:

Family & Friends
We would just like to let you
know that you are always welcome
to join in our social activities.
Some of the events you might like
to attend with your friend or
relative are
SING A LONG
CARPET BOWLING
CURRENT EVENTS
HAPPY HOUR
PUB
BINGO
Please check the schedules for
days, times and locations –
SEE YOU THERE!

Past and present joys were recaptured during the weekly sing-a-long and residents' choir practice, most often lead by a volunteer, a retired music teacher putting her talents to good use. Every special event day was celebrated. Bowling, fitness classes, even massage therapy were available. New, inventive ideas were always a surprise:

PICTURE GALLERY
We thought it would be fun to
have a display of old photographs
for the month of March. So we
would like to ask staff, residents
and families and volunteers to
lend us any old photos you might have.

- People pictures
- Old pictures of Vancouver or other parts of Canada
- Baby or wedding pictures
- My favorite animals pictures!

Anything you like!
Please drop photos off in Sally's office.
PLEASE DO JOIN IN
THANK YOU!!!

There was something for everyone. This was the "Royal Way," a fitting name I thought. The inner structure of staff activities, conveniences and care was also magnificent, as I was to discover.

It's no wonder that visitors often comment on how some care facilities are like hotels, with meals prepared, and maids to make the beds, and are puzzled if residents don't enjoy it to the full. As my tour continued, we greeted the residents. However, not all of them smiled and said hello. It was becoming evident that this residence was not entirely filled with joy. Its oldest resident was 103 and she was spoken of by many. As one elderly woman said, "I'm only 90, she is our example and our pride and joy." This was my introduction to the many months I would spend in this Home researching quality visiting. And I left that first day with a sense of anticipation.

VISITING RELATIVES' PERSPECTIVES

The Main Visitor: I have chosen as the main character, Edna, a woman who represents many relatives, perhaps like you, who have problems to confront as they attempt to fulfill the often exhausting role of "main visitor." Unfortunately the overriding theme of her portrait is not one of enjoyment.

Edna was an articulate, well-dressed woman of 61 years who lived only a few blocks from the care facility in which her 81-year-old mother resided. She had planned it that way, the location was not as convenient for some other visitors. Some of them were employed full time, some like Edna worked part-time and others were retired. One had young children, a husband, parents and a grandmother. Coming from a multi-generational family, she never had a minute for herself but managed to visit her grandmother once a week. She was truly a member of the Sandwich Generation (see Chapter 2).

But Edna typifies the main visitor. She was the daughter, lived closest to the facility and took her responsibility seriously. Nonetheless, these duties were not carried out without a price. She was the main link to the outside world, looking after legal matters, financial affairs, special purchases, sewing, mending and laundering. She transported her mother to and from medical appointments, attended to personal and business letters, kept herself informed of her mother's state of health and care and attempted to be intermediary between her mother and the physician. In all this she tried to be cheerful and bring some joy into her mother's life by bringing small gifts such as books and flowers to brighten the room. She said to me:

"My mother has been in this Home for three years. It took me at least a year to adjust to having her down the street. It's been an entirely different way of living. Before this, I was able to come and go whenever I pleased, on holidays or whatever. The first year was a very difficult period but now it has become a way of life. I have two daughters and five grandchildren, so if I want to take a holiday I ask my daughters to visit their grandmother. Other than that they never see her, the great grandchildren don't see her either even though they live quite close to her. I think my mother feels that nobody cares about her. She says, 'I never see my grandchildren or my great- grandchildren.' I went through a period when I would say to my kids, please go and see your grandmother and take the grandchildren. But they didn't want to go and so I am the only one who sees her. Also, I'm resentful towards my brothers. They both live on Vancouver Island and come to Vancouver only periodically. They might phone the odd time but do nothing else."

Typically, visitors became acquainted with other visitors in the Home and would stop to ask each other if they were experiencing similar concerns. One day, after a particularly distressing visit, Edna expressed her fear to me about how long this tormenting, stressful situation might continue. We both knew it could go on for years. As Edna walked through the front doors she saw a familiar face. She had seen this woman many times during the last three years. They had often said hello and commented on the weather. But this particular day Jane queried Edna's depressed look and after hearing her explanation, Jane stated that visiting was extremely difficult with her 88-year-old mother too. This is Jane's story:

Angry Visits: Jane, 58, still had a 19-year-old son at home and a husband to look after. Although she volunteered one day a week at the Home, she herself had Multiple Schlerosis and found it difficult to get around. Jane described a typical visit with her mother: *"When I enter my mother's room she's very happy to see me. I usually let her start to talk and she gets out all her complaints. When she finishes I say something but I usually don't say anything about her complaints. We have a little visit and I will take her out in the car if the sun is shining."*

"It's very poor visiting in the room. Over Christmas my visits consisted of taking her to the parties here where there's music and singing. She wouldn't go to unless she was dragged or really persuaded, so she often misses all that. Our visits are rather 'blah' anyway so I figure the time might as well be spent somewhere enjoyable, having tea or whatever. I used to visit her in the room but I found it depressing and quit doing that. If I went on a day that was decent I would take her outside to walk on the balcony. Taking her out in the car seemed like a real visit. But to sit in her room is no visit at all as far as I'm concerned. I don't know what she thinks of it. She never wants me to leave no matter how long I've been there."

"Ever since my mother has been in here I have not felt good about her. Since the social worker pointed out to me that I shouldn't feel guilty about not visiting and should only come when I felt like it, that's what I do. She doesn't hear so I yell all the time. She doesn't talk so I don't talk. When we're out with friends my mother refers to the Home as her 'rat hole.' She does not take part in activities and complains about everything, including me. Visiting has never been something that I enjoyed. I was doing it though, until I was told by a staff member 'You don't have to do that – do what you can comfortably do and forget it.' Before that I hated visiting and when I'd get home I'd be in a fair rage myself and take it out on my family. Now I realize that my mother is in a nice environment where there's lots of activities and lots of people and she's not being neglected in any way."

Those were the facts as Jane saw them and Edna felt better knowing that someone else had similar concerns. Edna had simply not thought to ask for professional help. Now she was prepared to do so.

Certainly, both these women were struggling with a myriad of issues. Jane was comforted by the professional help she received from the social worker, and Edna now was aware of this important service to family members. As for Jane, I don't know how aware she was of the anger in her voice. As I thought back on what she had described it was clear there were many things she could do differently to make visiting with her mother a more meaningful and satisfying time together. Why would she only take her mother out for a drive "if the sun is shining"? The mother had told me how much she enjoyed getting out – the weather was quite constant inside the Home– and most elderly people appreciate a change of environment.

I was disturbed about the issue of entertainment and music. Why did Jane's mother have to be "dragged" down to the party room? Was she resistant because she wanted her daughter "all for herself" for that precious visiting hour? Or was it because she could not hear the music and the crowd made her uncomfortable? Jane preferred being entertained when she visited her mother, but this did not take into account her mother's needs and desires.

As for the environment of the Home, Jane thought it was "nice," her mother called it her "rat hole" – an interesting name for a place Jane said had "lots of activities and lots of people and she's not being neglected in any way." Or did Jane feel she was neglecting her mother by visiting only once a week for an hour? She was a volunteer in the same Home one day a week and spent time with the other residents.

Clearly there were many unspoken issues between Jane and her mother. Here were two very unhappy women spending time together in a very unhappy way.

A Businessman's Visit: Dave was a 40-year-old businessman. He was married with no children. As the nearest relative, Dave had the responsibility to visit his 75-year-old mother and had found his own way to deal with visiting:

"When I get there and see that my mother's on a 'downer,' I don't stay long and I keep my visit short. When she's cheery and bright I stay longer because then the conversation lasts longer. That's the key – I read her mood, I don't try to force conversation, I just let her talk and I go from there. If she's on a 'downer,' she just wants to complain."

"I visit when it's convenient for me. I visit en route to and from home. I don't make a special trip to see her. I fit it in to my schedule. On a typical visit I talk with her, see what she has to say, try to get her to talk to me, see what she needs. I try to go more often and spend shorter periods of time instead of trying to draw it out. Fifteen minutes three or four times a week is better than one visit of an hour. She seems very happy to see me for a short period of time. Basically she tells me what's going on, and if she's had any news from her sister. I usually take her something like flowers to brighten up the room. I don't tell her things that are too difficult for her or things that I think she's going to have trouble remembering. I try to keep it pretty simple so she doesn't get confused, but I tell her if there's something I think she should know and I try to make sure she understands it before I leave. I take her out as much as I can. I find the way she

is now, she is only good for about a two hour period then she wants to go back. She may get upset and red in the face, but I don't give her much sympathy because the more I give her the longer she remains upset. I've found this out over the years. I just say, 'Oh, you'll be alright tomorrow.' Half the time she's not sick – she'll be good one minute and sick the next. When I take her out for dinner on Saturday or for Sunday brunch she might have an attack. She pretends that she's been shot in the head. I don't pay any attention to her; if I do pay attention to her then she'll do it again. I let her know later that I'm not pleased with that kind of dramatic behavior."

I couldn't help wondering what the mother's message really was. Dave was not about to look any deeper.

"There aren't any real difficulties with visiting. I try not to go at meal times and sometimes I just drop in to say hello and then I'm gone. She's not too interested in what I've done, so I have to listen. I don't do a lot of talking. If she has a problem then I suggest a solution to the problem."

For Dave, as for many visitors, the reason for visiting was a duty – as he put it: *"Just something I feel I should do. I make sure she's alright, I try to keep her interest up. The only thing I get out of visiting is seeing my mother cheerful and involved in something. That makes me feel better. I feel her problem is she doesn't do enough, she doesn't get involved in enough things. She has a tendency now to stay by herself too much. I'm happy when she's showing some interest in things – that's basically all I get out of it."*

Husband and Wife Visits: James, a 63-year-old businessman, visited his stepfather with his wife. Their visits illustrate further concerns:

"It's easier when both of us go. We bring some bran muffins or some small thing to eat, visit him in his room, talk with him, tell him the news of the family. We ask how he is and what's been happening and suggest he walk around a bit because we don't think he walks enough any more. Although he uses a cane, for his age, 88, he can walk fairly well. Then we go to the lounge: we always try to visit at tea time so that he's there with others. We talk to some of the residents and their visitors and observe how much he communicates with them. Afterwards we walk back to his room or try to persuade him to walk to the exit so that he has to walk back again. The main difficulty is that he doesn't communicate very well any more and I guess this is due to his lack of interest, his age and the fact that he doesn't get around as much any more. People therefore don't like to visit

him. My older daughter understands this, she's an R.N. But my younger daughter doesn't want to go at all."

This illustration depicts the situation for many visitors. Most of the effort has to be made by the visitors. The issue of communication is a major one. James reported that:

"My stepfather asks about a few people on occasion, but even things he used to be interested in have dropped by the wayside. When he was younger he never had a broad range of interests and this makes it more difficult to visit. Now we try to accompany him to the doctor because we feel that if he doesn't communicate with us he probably doesn't with the doctor. But we do get the feeling that he appreciates our efforts even though he doesn't say much. We get the feeling he enjoys our visits."

Sharing the Load: The Cameron visits came the closest to enjoyment. First, there were three relatives who shared the responsibility of visiting their 78-year-old father. Second, their relationship with him seemed to have always been a positive one. Third, the father's health was relatively good compared with the mother's, who had Alzheimer's Disease. They had spent seven years visiting her before she died. Compared to the visits with their mother, visiting with their father was, as Tom the son said, "a piece of cake, although we do have some difficulties with him too." This family did not usually visit together, but their views of visiting seemed to be similar. The following illustrates some common themes:

"Our visits are usually fairly short. Depending on what kind of a day Dad is having, it can be interesting or it can be very dull. Sometimes I can help him out if he's sitting waiting to be dressed, other times I just sit there. But I think all visits have value even if we sit there and say nothing. He always seems to be glad when we visit. He likes to show us his books or his new tapes, or he can talk about the Webster Show he watches every day, or the girl in the keep fit class. We mainly listen to his stories. He talks about a workshop in the basement that he'd like to use once his legs heal and he can get down there. He told us he had a lot of living to do."

When asked what they got out of visiting, Dick, the son-in-law said: *"It's a routine, it's a part of our life, I think we enjoy it."* Tom responded: *"Realistically, I'm fulfilling a responsibility. I visit because it's a responsibility, not because of my conscience. When I was a kid it was my responsibility to chop the wood. I'm still his son and now I have a different responsibility."* And the daughter commented: *"He likes to see us and we like to see him, that is the main reason we come. We know he wants to see us."* Tom added: *"Dad is confined – he can't go anywhere – he likes us to come to see him. The fact that he likes our company is what makes the visit. If we've not been around for a week or so he'll phone and say, 'Did you phone me – was that you who just phoned?'"*

What became clear to me as I talked to the visitors was a general lack of understanding. Visiting relatives seemed to think that what might be good for them, if they were in their parents' situation, might be altogether different from what the elderly persons wanted.

Key to Quality Visiting: The following are examples of what some relatives thought was the key to a quality visit.

1. "The biggest thing is just being there. My mother likes to tell her friends that I visit – that's the key. I could walk in and walk out the door and I think she'd still be pleased. She likes to show off her son."
2. "If I could sit long enough to listen to his stories that would make the visit for him. The two grandchildren are very patient when they visit. They listen to him – he likes to reminisce. He's interested in current events also and he'll relate what was happening when he was working in the General Hospital. The last visit, I was here for one and a half hours – he talked about himself the whole time and he was very interesting."
3. "If her frame of mind is good – it's a good visit. She has a tendency to bring you down with her, that's why I don't stay very long. I get down when I'm with her and have to get out. She and I have been fighting for years. We've always argued back and forth. I don't think that will ever change, but it's got less and less because I tolerate more. I try to ride the tide and not force any issues."

RESIDENTS – THE INSIDE STORY

The perceptions of visiting from the standpoint of the elderly residents take a different slant. Some residents have difficulty in expressing their views on visiting, and their experiences are not always pleasant or positive. The relationship with their relative is usually not ideal. Naturally they are reluctant to admit this, being more concerned with "keeping up a good front." For example, they often make excuses as to how busy their visitor is or that they must have been out of their room when their relative called. On the other hand, they often share things openly and freely, just as strangers do under difficult circumstances. Such intimacy is hard to believe and I was surprised, more often than not, at the degree of confidence and trust they seemed to have in me.

When elderly persons are institutionalized they usually live in the institution for the rest of their lives. For many of them, it was apparent that their days (months or years) were numbered and that they were beginning to withdraw, if they had not already done so. During my conversations with them, some respondents revealed their wish to die. "I feel I have lived a full life," said one woman of 87. "I'm just so tired of living," said another. Others conveyed this message by their lifestyle and behavior. As I was to discover, one elderly woman had talked of suicide. Discussing visiting with many of the residents was like discussing the last "hope of human kindness."

Mrs. Pink and Martha: Mrs. Martha Heatherington was born in 1896. She was a sad, lonely woman. Her room was decorated simply: no radio, no TV and the phone was seldom used. The artificial flowers stayed in bloom year round. A few old snapshots of family members topped the small dresser. Her room looked out on blossoming shrubbery that lined a walking path and just beyond it, a tall wire fence. Everything seemed to protect the residents from the outside world. "Did you fill in the sign-out sheet, Mrs. Heatherington?" the receptionist would have to yell. True, her memory was failing and she was very hard of hearing, but she had never signed a sheet when leaving her former home. There was good reason for it now and in fairness to the staff, they took their responsibilities seriously, but I don't know if this is what the residents wanted.

Many of the other residents' rooms were nicely decorated. My hunch was that these people decorate their room with the same amount of thought and energy that they were putting into living. The woman across the hall from Martha had pink walls, pink curtains, pink bedspread, pink china flowers. She dressed in a bright pink dress and her pink meticulously-made-up face covered many of the signs of aging. She went to great lengths to maintain her youthful look.

These two women, Martha and "Mrs. Pink," living as neighbors rarely saw each other and conversed even less frequently. They were two unique individuals with little in common. It's interesting that the visiting relatives wanted to instigate friendships in the Home. Was this to help their parents or to help themselves feel better?

Martha's main visitor was her daughter Jane, whose story we heard earlier on in this chapter. All of Martha's friends had died and there were no other family members who visited. I asked Martha to tell me about her visits with her daughter:

"Well, I can describe it this way to you. Every time that I have a visit with my daughter is a good time. In fact, as far as I'm concerned it's just the only time I live. I don't know what makes it a good time, we just come together and one is with the other and we talk. She has M.S. and it won't heal and she suffers. She keeps herself as busy as she can. She usually has a lot to talk about. She goes to church and she likes to sew. We just get together in no special way. We don't make things together, in fact we do very little – she is a very busy person and I'm not. We go out together in the car and sometimes for a little walk."

"I use my Bible a lot and I enjoy it – that's mostly what I do. I have never thought of myself as an interesting person in any way but I try to say to myself that there's lots of things I can do. I just can't seem to make the grade though. I've got so that I just want to be alone and that's not good. My daughter is very busy but I'm what you would call lazy. I'm very forgetful and I'm just ashamed and I can't help it. My head is not capable any longer."

It is revealing how Martha's perception of her visits differs from that of her daughter. Many elderly who spend a lot of time alone need to be provided with sensory stimulation such conversations can provide. Being alone can create or add to confusion and forgetfulness. There are numerous things you can do together during your visiting time. Suggestions for what to do together are discussed in Chapter 8.

Old people, such as Martha, are often self-critical. One useful technique for rebuilding self-esteem is reminiscing. You can encourage the person to talk about events in his/her life that indicate that his/her life is significant and still important.

Another elderly woman resident gave the following description of what she and her daughter did together and what they talked about:

"My daughter gets my knitting started for me and puts my clothes on. I'm blind in one eye and can only see a little out of the other so I have to count the stitches. We don't do very much together because she was her daddy's girl. At one time she never had any love for me at all because I was often in the hospital a month at a time and when I would come home she would do just as she wanted. I had pneumonia when she got married and couldn't give her the things she should have had and therefore she didn't think I was much of a mother. You can't do anything when you're in bed. We don't get too intimate. When we go for my corset she doesn't like me to be naked. We only had the one girl and it took me nine years to have her. She was her daddy's girl. Up until he died she was always with him, though she was good to me but not like a daughter. I ask my daughter what's she doing. She's my beneficiary. She has to do some of the

things but we have not been very close, mother and daughter, but she's a very good girl and likes to be on the go. I have a grand-daughter who's very close to me, however she lives in another area of the city and wants me to move closer."

Jack: Jack was 86 years old. Bare necessities in his room, no pictures on the walls. I suspected that, like many other elderly residents, he had never really adjusted to his new Home. His two sons were his only visitors and, like most businessmen, their conversation was not usually idle chatter. News of the family was the main topic of conversation as was the case for all of the residents. His sons were very fond of him and as Jack said, "they do everything to help me, their presence with me is all I expect. Coming in and sitting down and talking to me in here – that's their gift to me." He invited me to sit down on the bed beside him, as he was hard of hearing. We were not face to face, nor did he ever look my way. Jack had difficulty conversing with me and didn't initiate any comments.

I wasn't sure why he had agreed to talk to me. Possibly it was because he didn't want to say no to the activity director, who was so good to him. This was at least one thing he could do in return for her many kindnesses. I couldn't help but feel the sense of residents' vulnerability. In a very real way, most of these residents were at the mercy of the staff and their relatives. Most of them seemed very complacent, as if they had to accept whatever they got or didn't get, without question. If they weren't kind to the staff they might not get washed that day.

Dorothy: In contrast to many of the other residents, Dorothy had packed 87 years of living into her small quarters. Possibly she hadn't unpacked yet – I wasn't quite sure. She had everything she needed and, more importantly, everything she wanted around her. Her past had been rich and full and she still had a zest for living every day and every minute. Her interest in people and the world around her was evident. She had been that way all her life, and the twinkle in her eye revealed very clearly that there was some mystery about her.

Dorothy had been blessed with good health, although now she was very hard of hearing and said it was a terrible nuisance. She had been to church last weekend and spoke of the individual speakers in the pews. "I could actually hear the music and it was wonderful." She required a daily dose of oxygen and enjoyed a shot or two of whisky. As the Home's only "fortune teller," I can only imagine what she said was in store for some of the other residents. She loved bingo, bridge, clothes, and especially flowers and said, "The happiest times are when people walk in here with flowers." She loved to read, was a fiend for TV and enjoyed baking in the residents' kitchen. Walking was also a favorite activity but more than anything else she loved to visit.

Dorothy, as you might well have guessed, had many visitors. Her face glowed as she described one of her regular visits:

"Every Wednesday my sister comes and takes me out to lunch to the same place. We go to the mall, have lunch and a little drink. Then we shop. I get all my clothes there as I have a charge account and I can take her out for lunch. It's a very nice visit when I can do something for someone. I like to discuss with my family bits of good news or something that's helped somebody when they've been to visit me. A good visit is when someone tells me something good that's happened to them or when someone makes me feel good after they've gone. I've never had a bad visit – I haven't got a bad friend. I reminisce a great deal. I used to fish a lot and shoot, too, when I was younger. I remember one cold day I got my 'limit' while my husband was lighting the fire. It's very good to reminisce, you can forget your aches and pains."

Dorothy had a wonderful sense of humor and had obviously enjoyed telling me this story. I had enjoyed listening and was convinced she drew her family and friends into her life just as she had me, through these tales of yesteryear.

Almost all of these residents seemed ripe for the fruits of "life review," a process that for the elderly involves reminiscing about past experiences in order to cope or adapt to present situations. It was apparent that the relatives were not conscious of this task, nor had enough skills to work through it. (See Chapter 6).

The majority of these residents were over eighty years of age. Most of their contemporaries had died as well as many of their own children. Although Dorothy was a unique person in this setting, her losses were typical. Her husband had died some years ago and, within the past few months, she had lost her son, a grandson, her daughter and her brother's wife. But life went on for Dorothy. She somehow made things happy for herself and everyone around her.

Dorothy's Advice for Visitors: Advice for visitors? Sure! Don't let people get old. Try to get them talking. People like to talk and tell you things. Tell visitors to talk to the people they're visiting but not in a way that they're feeling sorry for them. Some people think that because you're in a Home, you're without everything including money. Visitors have got to give something of themselves to the older person. Be bright and happy try to make them feel that you're glad to see them. Don't go in looking mournful. I think that would be very depressing.

Often when people come in to visit, they are very nervous, even your own friends, and they sometimes don't tell you all the truth about things. They want to shelter you but eventually you do find out. And the reason they didn't tell you is because they thought it would affect you in some way. It's not helpful to protect us because we all feel normal. I'm 87. I feel maybe time is passing pretty quickly – I want to live as long as I can, I want to enjoy everything I can and I want everybody to treat me like I was when I was 20 or 25.

Lack of "Fit" Although the environment, as many of the residents reported, met their physical and social needs, what about their emotional needs? Could the visiting relatives provide this kind of support? Not if they were unaware. Visiting institutionalized elderly is, after all, mainly unexplored territory.

This particular generation of elderly residents, the oldest born in 1895, the youngest in 1917, had been concerned throughout their lives with "survival." Their adult children, on the other hand, had attempted to "save." The grandchildren and great-grandchildren seemed to be more concerned with "spending." Philosophies and values, the residents' needs and the relatives' help, were often far apart. The elderly residents didn't usually articulate their desires or wishes. And when they did the relatives were often either not motivated to respond, lacked knowledge of the situation or lacked the necessary skills. Some elderly were accepting of their circumstances, while others made unrealistic demands of their main visitors. What the elderly valued most was to be treated as normal, to know that they were cared about and to have contact with their families. Most of the residents were very lonely and many of them articulated this fact. The visiting relatives were caring individuals who were helping their elderly relative in their own way. *Help as seen from the relatives perspective, however, was not always regarded as meaningful by the resident.* In other words, it wasn't necessarily the type of caring or help that the elderly needed or wanted.

A daughter and her 82-year-old mother provide a good illustration. At her frequent visits to the care facility, the daughter had continued to try to get the life-long affection and approval that she felt she'd never had. She was doing everything she could think of to help her mother. The visits usually ended in extreme frustration and depression as the daughter felt helpless, hopeless and at times abused. With a great deal of emotion the daughter reported:

"When I go to visit my mother she says things to me in an angry voice like, 'where have you been, I've been waiting for you all morning?'" This daughter had never had a good relationship with her mother. Now she felt guilty and was trying very hard to "please."

The mother, on the other hand, had reported: *"My daughter comes to visit me when she can. She's very busy. She tries to do many things for me, wants me to go out in the car and shopping for a new dress. I'm very tired, I'm tired of living. I've seen all the parks and flowers before and I don't need any new clothes. She doesn't need to come as often as she does – she's very busy anyway."* This mother was attempting, by herself, to bring closure to her life. Why couldn't they work on this difficult life task together? Probably because relatives find it very difficult to cope with the physical and mental changes in their elderly parents. In some cases they hardly recognize them as the same persons they once knew.

To walk a mile in someone else's shoes, vicariously experiencing the feelings, thoughts and experiences of another, is a difficult task when few pathfinders have marked the way. Some people have never learned to give empathy, and feelings of frustration make it hard to empathize. Possibly it is easier to empathize with younger age groups because we have "been there" in one way or another. We have not been old. But we have either spent time in hospitals, or have gone for brief times without the use of a limb, or have had handicaps or disabilities to cope with. We have felt loss when a friend or relative has died. So we are equipped to empathize more than we might realize.

Without empathy and effective communication neither the relatives' or residents' needs are met and these circumstances lead to frustrating visits. The visitors attempt to help in their way and very often the needs and wants of the elderly are missed. It is a high expectation and, as often as not, an unrealistic one that relatives should know how to help an old person. Chapter 5 lists suggestions intended to help you become an effective visitor.

Before beginning this research I had experienced the stresses and strains of visiting: visiting with my own father in an institution, living through his emotional pain, trying desperately to help him, attempting to review his life, to have it all make some sense to both of us. Those days were filled with fear and profound sadness. At the Royal Way Care Home, I had walked into the lives of the elderly residents and their relatives and now I was walking out. What did I conclude from my visits?

The residents' physical and mental health was a major factor in the quality of the visits. When mental and physical changes take place, the nature of visiting changes.

Healthier residents generally seemed happier. They were more interested and involved in life, had more visitors and their visitors had "easier" visits. Also, residents who were more "outgoing" had more visitors than the residents who were withdrawn. Regular "healthy" visits add quality to the lives of the elderly in institutions.

Almost all of the residents wanted to talk and to visit in the interview. The majority of the residents had only one main visitor, usually a family member. They seemed hungry for companionship and needed to feel cared about. They enjoyed being interviewed, possibly because it fulfilled both these needs. Listening to complaints is difficult for relatives, but, it does seem to benefit the resident, allowing them to "let off steam."

The portraits in this chapter capture essential features of the residents' environment, relatives' visits, individual characteristics, their relationships, values and perceptions. All these things have a bearing on the quality of visits. The physical and mental abilities of most of these elderly residents gradually grow dimmer; nonetheless, they are important human beings. What they wanted most of all was to have someone care about them, to be treated as a person, and to have contact with their families.

5
Suggestions For Visiting

One of the big challenges in being involved in the life of an elderly resident is being an effective visitor. Most people have not been taught anything about visiting, nor do they realize the numerous issues that they need to consider. Nevertheless, it's a fact that visiting the elderly in long term care facilities is with us to stay. The purpose of this chapter is to improve the time you spend with your elderly relative. Visiting in nursing homes can be very artificial; it differs from short-stay hospital visiting. "Long term" visiting will be a regular part of your life for many years to come.

WHAT IS A VISIT?

Let's start by defining the word. "Visit" in *Webster's Dictionary* is described as: a short stay, a brief residence as a guest, to go to see in order to comfort or help, to pay a call on as an act of friendship or courtesy, to chat, converse. *Roget's Thesaurus* defines "visit" as drop in, call, look in on. In Watt and Calder's book, *Taking Care*, the authors state that "visit" may sometimes be an inappropriate word as it suggests friendliness, sharing, talking, companionship and laughter. For one reason or another visits can be unpleasant experiences. Visiting is often just a matter of "being present." It is for you to discover what "visit" means to you, to help you come to terms with the over-riding purpose of your own visits.

You may already be applying numerous ideas and suggestions listed in this chapter, but many will give you new ways of looking at visiting time. Improving the circumstances surrounding visits, enhancing interaction during actual visiting time and altering your expectations will improve the quality of visiting for you and your elderly relative. The attitude of "putting in time" is destructive. Some elderly feel they are just putting in time and, if you both are, your visit will be meaningless. If you really want to spend time with your elderly relative (and you won't be fooling anyone if you don't) the following pages and Chapters 6, 7, and 8 will be of particular interest. If you don't want to visit but have decided that you are going to, you can start considering what the word means to you and how important "connecting" with your elderly relative really is.

REASONS FOR VISITING

Marge was a 79-year-old woman who "rented" a small space in a care facility. Or was this actually room and board? We seldom think of facilities this way, but indeed, she was paying rent, it was her turf and more importantly Marge called it "home." She spent most of her time in her room, by herself. Almost blind, no longer able to read or watch TV, and having been told that a hearing aid would not help her type of hearing loss, the quality of her life was diminishing. "I'm a jack of all trades, master of none," Marge told me, "I have worked hard all my life. To end up like this!"

No one visited Marge; most of her friends had died. She commented on what a terrific companion the nursing home cat was. "You have no idea about loneliness, it's like living in Siberia." "Do you mean it's like being in jail?" I asked. Marge responded, "Jail, my dear, would be a welcome relief. At least in there you would have someone to talk to."

Clearly, we do not need a scientific study to know that visiting promotes well-being and eases adjustment to nursing home life. The regular contact of family and friends benefits the elderly person because of the extra stimulation it provides. It is also appreciated by the staff, who find the relatives' interest encouraging and shows them that the resident is cared about and can ease workloads. Visiting also gives the opportunity for relatives to work for better quality of life in care facilities.

Why visit?

Visiting alleviates loneliness, aimlessness, boredom, apathy, and feelings of insecurity.

Visiting provides company, friendship, support and help.

Visiting is crucial unless society is satisfied with treating old people as socially dead. Studies show us that the elderly feel the most important issue is a continuation of ties with people that add quality to their lives.

Visiting helps break the monotony, adds meaning to endless days and enriches life.

Visiting helps the elderly adjust to group living and a lack of privacy.

Visiting stimulates physical and mental health and helps alleviate concerns about failing health and the future.

Visiting may help the elderly to forget their troubles or put their concerns and problems into perspective. Family and friends can help old people review a philosophy that involves the realities of life, pain, suffering and death. These are issues that are side-stepped. Two people can work things through better than one.

Visiting helps develop feelings of achievement when sharing in activities.

Visiting helps to improve your relative's satisfaction with living by your encouragement, interest and participation in nursing home life.

Visiting gives elderly people moments of happiness.

Visiting can help heal the sorrows of the past and can bring joy and laughter, as humorous stories are shared.

Help: As the old refrain goes, "Don't Bring Me Posies, It's Shoesies I Need." The balance between helping and hindering is hard to find because we are all so different. Your relationship to the elderly person is not like anyone else's. "Help" is usually centered on needs – two sets of needs – the elderly person's and yours.

The elderly experience the same hierarchy of needs as anyone else: 1) physiological; 2) safety; 3) belongingness and love; 4) esteem; 5) self-actualization. The lower more basic needs must be satisfied before the next level can be satisfied. The needs of the elderly are not much different than any other generation. We all need food, a roof over our heads, love, affection, intimacy, help when we're sick, ways to feel good about ourselves, to be useful and feel needed, to give to others, to be active, challenged, to achieve, to be creative, to feel joy, to laugh and to fill spiritual needs. The fulfillment of these needs is what lends to quality in our lives. In order to contribute and add meaning to life we need to help the elderly meet their needs. We can often find out what these needs are by putting ourselves in their shoes, by observing, by really listening.

It is important to make sure you are helping at the "right" level. Bringing food when what is needed is affection, is not helpful. To help them use their creative talents, when what they need to feel is that they belong and are still part of the family, is not helpful.

Help is worthwhile only when it is meaningful or useful to the person receiving it. Advice-giving, avoiding, denying, punishing, and controlling are not helpful and do not add quality to life. It is necessary, therefore, to work towards mutual acceptance and mutual growth, trust, openness, problem-solving, and exploring things together.

In an effort to help our elderly relatives and show them we care we tend to do many things for them like brushing their hair or shaving. Under some circumstances this is necessary but in others it may rob the elderly person of an opportunity to maintain a little independence and dignity. Finding the middle road between helping and hindering is important. If one of your goals is to encourage independence, you're on the right track. You can do this in many ways. Here are a few suggestions:

- arranging a more manageable environment: a clock that's easy to read, a mirror with a solid base, drawers that are organized;
- buying or sewing clothing that is suited to what the person needs: velcro fasteners instead of buttons or zippers, slippers that are easy to put on;
- encouraging the person to practice and learn to eat with their "good" hand – the one that isn't paralyzed.

Most people would like to do things for themselves. You may want to set some goals now, keeping in mind what you have just read. Your goals might be:

1. To encourage your relative to do as many tasks as possible and offer support only when really necessary;
2. To encourage participation in some physical activities with you, or if that is not feasible, some mentally stimulating games;
3. To bring friendship, love and affection whenever possible;
4. To be involved and participate in the activities of the Home;
5. To minimize handicaps or disabilities in order for the elderly to live a full life;
6. To stimulate an interest in other people and in the outside community by sharing information and encouraging activities and interests outside of the Home;
7. To be involved in mutual goal setting with your relative, which will enhance his or her sense of control and reinforce dignity and self-esteem.

You may have other goals for yourself or perhaps you may want to choose two or three of these goals – write them down on a piece of paper and stick them on your fridge. Remember, you will need to consider the uniqueness and needs of your own relatives for them to benefit from your time together. When you succeed, your contribution will add quality to the elderly persons' life.

STRUCTURING THE VISIT

In all things, success depends upon
Previous preparation,
And without such preparation
There is sure to be failure.
– Confucious

2:30 Tuesday afternoon. Mrs. Eileen Davidson is getting ready for her daily visit to the nursing home where her mother of 96 has resided for the past five and a half years. She, like thousands of other women and men who visit regularly, has many things to consider. Eileen is now an experienced visitor and for the most part has learned the hard way.

Eileen is the only daughter still living and she herself is 75. "It all depends on how you look at things," Eileen would say. "I only feel 45." That was a good indication that she had lots of living left to do, as well as the right attitude, energy and spirit. Not only that, Eileen had discovered an important secret to enjoying time with her mother: structuring the visit.

Each nursing home has policies and regulations about visiting. It will have a brochure giving information about the variety of services, activities, costs, and so forth. Please refer to Chapter 3 for further details. Familiarize yourself with the information specific to *your* nursing home.

Visiting, like any other important event, takes preparation, planning, creativity and imagination. Often family members and friends get into a deadly routine when visiting their loved ones. Making even one change in your daily or weekly visits can make the visiting experience more satisfying for everyone.

Planning: When planning your visit you should decide, mutually if possible, what day you are going to visit. Also, try to determine what time of day is best.

Location of visit: You may want to think ahead of time about where you'll visit. Better still, ask the elderly person's preference:

- resident's room
- lounge
- garden
- corridors
- sundeck
- solarium
- your home
- your car
- restaurant

One common complaint from visitors is the lack of private places to meet. As one person said: "You never know who's going to walk into the room when my husband and I are visiting. We may just want a quiet time together without any disruptions. There is no opportunity for intimacy since he has been here." If this is a concern of yours you will need to discuss this with the head nurse, director of care, or a social worker. They are there to help you.

Timing:

Better late than never, but better never late.

Waiting for a visitor can seem endless for an elderly person in a nursing home. It is therefore especially important to be on time. Some elderly tire easily; their health and mood can vary from day to day. If you can decide mutually when to visit, that is best. For many people their work lives dictate when the visit will take place. If your time is flexible ask the elderly person when they would like to be visited. Some have particular rest times, special events and favorite television programs. Try to arrange visits around these if possible.

Meal times

For some, meal times are an excellent time to visit particularly if your relative needs help while eating. Otherwise meal time may not be best, as this is a time that might be enjoyed with other residents. It is wise to check with the staff about the most appropriate time as you may be unaware of the effects your visit has on your relative.

Weekends

Weekends can be an especially good time as often there are fewer activities and fewer staff. Weekend days may be even longer and more lonely than regular weekdays. Visiting takes a lot of energy. It's better not to visit when you're tired.

Regularity, Frequency and Duration: Commitment to visiting is crucial and regular visits are important for a number of reasons. Studies show that residents who are visited more frequently appear to receive more attention from staff. To an elderly person your visiting appointment is as important as your own doctor's appointment. If you have to change the time of your visit remember to call the elderly person or the nursing home staff. It's common courtesy and very important. It can be very disappointing and frustrating to an elderly person if your visits are erratic. People visit once a day, two or three times a week, once a week and so forth. Occasional visiting is often more disappointing than beneficial to an older person, but don't be too hard on yourself if you must change a visiting time; just phone the home and let your relative know what happened and when you'll be coming.

Frequent visiting keeps you informed of your relative's situation and enables you to be an advocate ensuring quality care. Frequent visits of a half or one hour's duration are often better for residents, especially those who tire easily. Some visitors stay for a longer period. Make it clear to your relative at the beginning of your visit how long you will be staying. This will help you later if you find it difficult to leave or if your relative wants you to stay longer than you can.

En route: Do you try to prepare yourself for the particular mood your elderly parent or spouse may be in? They may typically be having a "good day" or a "bad day." You won't know until you get there what kind of day they're having. However, if you prepare yourself for the possibility of a "bad one," your chances of having a good visit will be greater.

It is important for you to try to get yourself into the right frame of mind. Feeling nice thoughts, remembering some kindnesses your parents did for you, looking at fresh spring blossoms on the trees, thinking of something humorous or taking an alternative route all help to set a pleasant tone. And when you get there you may be able to open a conversation with something like: "a funny thing happened to me on the way to . . ." that could lift the mood.

What to Take: Should I take something? Many people say it's not necessary to take anything but a pleasant smile and yourself. I believe, however, that it is very important to take something. It could be something as simple as a snapshot, a piece of artwork one of the grandchildren has drawn at school, a clump of colorful leaves, the first blossom of spring or a homemade cookie. It tells them they're important enough to do a little extra for (see Chapter 8, section on Gifts, for more suggestions). Keep a "surprise box" at home and fill it with things you come across, so you can pick one out before you go visiting. If you visit daily or two or three times a week you don't need to take something for each visit.

Your Actual Time Together: Where shall we visit? In the small lounge, the cafeteria? Shall we go for a ride in the car, to the park or have a picnic lunch on the nursing home grounds? These are only some of the many questions to answer that will increase your chances of enjoying your time together. For many elderly, a change is indeed better than a rest. People living in nursing homes have plenty of time to rest. The most important part of visiting is spending quality time together. By implementing some of the suggestions in this book you will be able to really "live the visit."

Taking Leave: At times it might be hard to wind up a visit. Tell your relative or friend when you will see them again. Don't make promises unless you know you can keep them. It is distressing to an elderly person to hear things like: "As soon as we get a nice sunny day I'll take you out for a drive through the park." Elderly persons have the same climate every day – often sterile and bleached clean. Besides, if you make promises like this one and live in a wet climate, you may never be able to fulfill your promise. Not all people dislike the rain: it's lovely and fresh and makes flowers blossom and bushes smell good.

Elderly people look forward to your visits much more than you might realize. Some want you to stay longer no matter how long you visit. Many visitors just stick it out until someone or something "comes up." If you have always lingered and not known how to terminate your time together you might want to consider doing it differently. That doesn't mean it will be easy – sometimes it's just a matter of making a small change in an out-dated habit – often it helps to leave the elderly person with something to look forward to for the next visit. Not necessarily something tangible. You may say that you anticipate them telling you some information about a coming event in the home, that you really care that their arm will be better. Or you will look up something for them, you will tell them about the book you've read or the concert you've been to.

If it is comfortable for you and your relative, your last gesture before you walk out could be a caring touch, a squeeze of the hand, or better still a real live hug. "See you Thursday afternoon Mom, at three."

What to do After a Difficult Visit: Visiting in a long-term care facility can be depressing. And let's face it, for some, it's a real chore. It is important to look after yourself, particularly when you have a disturbing or frustrating time while visiting. Have some plan in mind for these days. Coffee with a friend, a little shopping spree, a walk in the park. A movie immediately after a difficult visit helps to get you back on track. This is when your imagination can help. Use it to think of ways that will make you feel better.

POTPOURRI OF VISITING SUGGESTIONS

Don't start anything you're not prepared to carry through.

Don't talk about personal matters in the hallways. Information may be overheard, misinterpreted and could sound like gossip.

Dress with zest.

Act in a kind and friendly manner.

You are not expected to solve all the problems of your elderly relative. The nurse, social worker, pastor, doctor, or lawyer can help you.

Respect the dignity of the elderly and their privacy. Regard them as individuals with their own identities.

Remember to call other elderly residents in the home by name. This can mean a great deal to the old person.

If there are elderly residents who don't have any visitors, you may be able to help the staff find a visitor for them.

An advertisement I'd like to see some day:

QUALIFIED VISITORS WANTED

Nursing Homes invite applications for qualified visitors. We have immediate openings. The successful candidate will visit to ensure that maximum quality of life is achieved for their elderly relative. Other duties include: taking your elderly parent, spouse or friend home for a visit if possible; participating in activities and special events; and going on outings arranged by the Home. This job has arisen because of the ongoing need for the elderly to have meaningful contact. These visitors will help the older person feel like they belong and are still important.

Minimum requirements for this new and challenging position include: confidence, good communication skills, good health, dependability, empathy, sense of humor, resourcefulness, creativity, time, knowledge of Nursing Home regulations, respect for elderly persons.

Transportation an asset but not necessary. No previous experience needed. The incumbent will be responsible to him/herself only.

Remuneration: Our salary and benefit package is consistent with other visitors across the country who believe it is more blessed to give than to receive.

If you're looking for a challenging opportunity, not just a job, reply in writing to Qualified Visitors Inc. No martyrs please.

TYPES OF VISITORS

Paid Visitors: People are wrong when they say "money can't buy happiness." Family members who live far away can hire a "special" person to spend time with their elderly relative. Furthermore, a paid visitor could supplement your visiting time. There are agencies that provide companion service at an hourly rate. Some visiting relatives hire someone to visit their aging parent or spouse while they are away on holidays. Even if you don't go out of town you still need a break at various times from daily or weekly visiting. You may have relatives or friends of friends who would like a part-time job visiting your relative. If you plan to have a paid companion check with the head nurse as to the Home's policy.

Barter Visitors: You might be able to trade some visiting time with a friend or neighbor. For instance, if you have a particularly busy week and can't seem to get to the Nursing Home, you could offer to look after your friend's children in exchange for your friend visiting your mother. Possibly the ultimate barter would be "trade visits" – your mother for mine. This could work well in the case of difficult visits when relationships are tense and stressful. A change might make your own situation look easier.

Surprise Visitors: On occasion it is a nice surprise to just drop in for a brief ten minute hello. It is important that you tell your relative "I'm en route to an appointment and wanted to stop in for ten minutes to let you know I was thinking about you." Take your coat off, sit down, have a little chat and keep the promise you've made to yourself. After ten minutes, get up and leave. Surprise visitors can make the day for a resident.

The Clergy: Even if one has not had a life-long affiliation with a religious institution, clergy can play an important role to older persons in care facilities. Many nursing homes have their own clergy or trained pastoral visitors who bring renewed courage and cheer. A visit from one's own minister, priest or rabbi can give real peace of mind to the elderly. Taped services, and news from friends in the congregation are always welcome. A closing prayer can give great comfort. Aging brings a series of losses, many of which are irreplaceable. It is very important to know that one of the few things a person never has to give up or lose is their faith.

The Doctor: Doctors have a responsibility to visit their elderly patients regularly to check their current state of health and give reassurance. If your elderly relative can no longer get to the physician's office, make an appointment for the doctor to visit. Physicians often need to be encouraged to maintain contact with their elderly patients.

The Lawyer: Although lawyers need not necessarily make routine visits, it is important that the elderly person knows that his or her affairs are in order. If appropriate have the lawyer pay a short visit or make a phone call. Before the lawyer calls or visits be sure to check the cost and the nursing home policy regarding who can witness documents, etc.

Volunteers: There have been many pamphlets written for the "Volunteer Visitor." The information in this book applies to all persons involved with the elderly: professionals, family, friends, volunteers, students and so forth. Volunteers often become substitute family members. A most important rule for anyone participating in the life of an elderly person is to treat them as you would a good friend. Volunteers fill a great need as elderly residents often have no family or friends living nearby. If you don't live in the same city as your relative, write to the administrator of the nursing home for information about volunteer visitors.

VISITING BY MAIL - Red Letter Days

Consider the postage stamp:
Its usefulness consists of the ability
To stick to one thing till it gets there
– Josh Billings

Visiting by mail is important even if you live in the same city. It can be a welcome relief to the routine of nursing home life. Notes or letters, however, should be used not as a substitute but as a complement to visits. They take less than fifteen minutes to write even when you take a little extra care to write legibly with dark ink on light paper.

Mail shows that you're interested and you care about the person. Mail is something to read, to be entertained by, to think about, to share with staff or relatives or friends in the Home, to answer and to read again and again. Some elderly people have saved letters from the past filled with accolades from friends or colleagues as well as kindnesses bestowed. Reading these letters again with the elderly boosts their self-esteem and can give you added insight into their lives. There are numerous items you can send through the mail. Small bouquets of flowers make excellent surprises (see "What to Take" section for other suggestions). It doesn't have to cost anything – it could be an article from the newspaper or a child's drawing.

Greeting cards: Greeting cards brighten up long days. Avoid shiny paper and look for easy-to-read lettering. If you don't have a lot to say or don't know what to say, imagine you are having a little conversation.

News of your family, friends and activities are always of interest. An encouraging thought such as: "I remember the lovely baking you brought to my daughters' graduation reception. You are always so thoughtful!" is a nice way to finish. Enclosing a newsclipping adds interest to a short letter. Frequent, short letters are nicer than one long letter at Christmas time.

Someone I know has lunch once a week with her sister in Africa. She goes out for lunch to a restaurant near her office and writes a letter while she eats, a pleasant break from her busy day and appreciated news and contact for her sister. You could treat yourself to lunch while writing a note to your elderly relative in a nursing home.

Lastly, letters can be used to tell your elderly parent, relative or friend how much they mean to you. Many people don't ever tell their parents how they really feel about them (sometimes it's just as well they don't). If you do love your parents and appreciate what they have done and may still be doing for you it's better to tell them in a letter than not to tell them at all.

Post cards: Post cards can be sent from in town as well as out of town. A friend of mine sent his 79-year-old aunt a postcard from England while he was holidaying there. The picture was of a woman with a mohawk hairdo, half shaved head and purple hair. Crazy and fun. His aunt had that card on her bulletin board for a year. It made a good conversation piece for other visitors who came to see her.

VISITING BY PHONE

Long Distance: A long distance phone call for residents who have a phone in their room and who can hear well over the phone can be very meaningful. Some elderly people, however, do not enjoy telephone conversations as they may think it is not a "wise" way to spend money. It is therefore a good idea to keep the call short, share a bit of family news, a job promotion, tell them you're thinking about them, and give them something to look forward to: "Linda is sending you a picture of her graduation."

Short Distance: Perhaps you use the phone for keeping in touch with your elderly parent on a daily basis. If this is a good arrangement for you, fine. If it's a burden you can change this routine to every other day or twice a week. Let your relative know why you are making the change: "I've taken a part time job" or "I'm too rushed in the morning," or "I have to take Nancy to her swimming lessons three times a week." When you make the calls less of a burden you'll be amazed at how their quality improves. Phoning is a nice complement to visiting, but there's no substitute for visiting in person.

THE BENEFITS OF VISITING TO YOU

Getting involved in the life of elderly residents also has benefits to you, helping to relieve feelings of guilt or remorse. Visiting helps you feel good about yourself while giving to others. Participating in nursing home life may help you feel better and more assured about your elderly relative's new Home. Knowing that your relative's physical needs are being met might alleviate stress and thus allow you more energy to put into emotional support. It promotes the learning of:

- patience;
- the aging process;
- communication skills, especially listening;
- organizational and leadership skills;
- life through the experience of others;
- skills for future employment, and

The opportunity to:

- perform on a musical instrument, in drama;
- share skills: teach art, painting or creative drama;
- have your own needs met – and to feel needed.

CONCLUSION

Past relationships and communication skills are major factors in determining quality visits, and, when these factors are recognized and nurtured, visiting experiences will undoubtedly improve.

"Quality" visiting involves three key groups: the visitors, the residents and the professionals. All must interact in a meaningful way. Visitors are a potent catalyst for changing visits and experiencing them in different and improved ways. Visitors are also human beings, vulnerable, fearful, frail and often elderly themselves. It is in recognizing these human qualities that the structures of change must be organized.

A CHECKLIST FOR REVIEWING YOUR VISITS

1. Are you enjoying any part of visiting?

2. Do you feel good about visiting?

3. What is the best part of visiting?

4. What is the worst part? What can you do to make it better?

5. Do you ever talk to other people who visit in the Home?

6. Have you thought of a taking a gerontology course to learn more about the aging process and the elderly?

7. Would you like to lead a visitors' support group in the Home?

8. Are you being "good" to yourself? Have you taken a break from visiting lately?

9. Have you thought of any ways to get others in the family to visit instead of feeling resentful for all that you do and they don't do?

10. Do you share your successful visits with other visitors?

You may want to write these questions and your answers in a notebook and check them from time to time.

This process must be centered on the needs and well-being of the institutionalized elderly.

Clearly, an essential ingredient for adding quality to the life of residents is appropriate methods of communication. Visitors need to communicate their willingness to visit, a desire to maintain ties and a caring attitude based on empathy and respect. They need to develop and express a great deal of patience – an understatement. Visitors need to communicate with the staff and to give them insights into the lives of their elderly relative in order to facilitate, at the highest level possible, the type of care the elderly person needs. They need to ask questions at the "right" time and of the "right" person (See Chapter 6 for more details). Their concerns and conflicts could be discussed with other visitors as well as with appropriate staff, friends or other professionals.

If visitors could express appreciation and give encouragement to the staff in proportion to the time they spend discussing concerns and complaints, a climate of greater mutual understanding and trust would ultimately benefit all parties. Visitors need to permit an equality of power by including the elderly person in decisions. This helps to create a sense of worth in the older person. A degree of commitment is necessary to acquire knowledge of the normal age-related changes that affect communication: hearing loss, vision loss, memory loss. This process establishes better rapport thereby adding meaning to visits. Also, a commitment to identify activities involving shared interests helps to facilitate a positive approach to visiting.

Often the timing and duration of visits must be dictated by the visitor. It is in structuring the visit that many problems may be overcome. Being clear about differing expectations of visitor and resident is important. Setting clear boundaries as to when the visit will take place, getting "in the mood" for a visit, planning an activity, or bringing a conversation piece could alter the focus of difficult interactions. Visiting in silence, just "being there" and an appropriate means of "taking leave" are also essential to visiting.

Most main visitors take responsibility for the type of visit and regardless of the quality of the relationship with their elderly relative, they are committed to their new roles. These visitors, however, receive few benefits from visiting. There is a definite lack of acknowledgement, encouragement, praise and thanks for the efforts they make for their elderly relative. The following quote from a daughter exemplifies this well: *"I was visiting my mother this morning and took her a dress all freshly washed and ironed – all my mother said was, 'Please hang it in the closet for me.'"* Another woman told me that she cancelled whatever she had scheduled in order to visit her sister when she was in need and never received a word of thanks for all she did.

The alert elderly person has responsibilities in the process of visiting as well. They have a responsibility to communicate their needs and wants and to express appreciation. They need to make themselves a part of decisions and help to create an atmosphere of mutual trust and understanding. It is fair for elderly persons to make realistic demands of the staff and of their visitors. Some old people do not express appreciation of the efforts put forth by their visiting relatives and the staff, as they become vulnerable, frail and withdrawn.

Staff members need to be familiar with the difficulties and stresses that visiting creates and give support and encouragement to the visitors. Special services with trained personnel also must be an integral part of the visiting experience. Social workers, other counsellors, and local family service agencies can facilitate communication and help resolve conflicts. Staff can also assist in helping to "normalize" the visits and to treat the residents' space with due respect.

Such factors as the environment in the Home, its proximity and location, time, frequency and duration of visits also affect the visit. Visiting relatives, residents and professionals speak about these factors, often because these topics are less threatening than discussions about relationships and death and dying. It is my perception that elderly residents think a great deal about these more profound issues and would be open to talking about and dealing with them rather than pretending they didn't exist.

What is a quality visit and how do we measure it? Feeling satisfied, fulfilled, worthwhile. Feeling that your time is well spent, that you are making a difference; as opposed to feeling helpless and hopeless. Realizing a sense of purpose, sensing that both you and your elderly relative feel good, using your sense of humor, having fun. All of these factors lead to mutual enjoyment.

The characteristics that we often admire in people of any age – kindness, generosity, openness, honesty and understanding – are the qualities that promote effective visits and add quality to life. Visiting demands an extraordinary amount of energy, creativity and imagination from everyone. Through meaningful interaction, all parties could experience more fulfillment. That, in fact, is the main purpose of "quality" visiting.

> *You are as young as your faith, as old as your doubt; as young as your self-confidence, as old as your fear; as young as your hope, as old as your despair.* – S. Ullman

6
Communicating

Break, break, break,
On thy cold gray stones, O Sea!
And I would that my tongue could utter
The thoughts that arise in me.
– Alfred Lord Tennyson

One of the greatest challenges faced by visiting relatives is developing new and different methods of communication. As we discovered in Chapter 2, the task of maintaining an "adult-to-adult" relationship with your elderly relative can be difficult – but when achieved, renders a more enjoyable time for all.

This Chapter is not intended as a detailed course on communication skills. Rather its purpose is to highlight some of the methods that you will need to employ if you want to increase the satisfaction and enjoyment of time spent with your elderly relative. Visiting, after all, is communicating in one form or another. It takes confidence as well as "know how" to make the human contact that will enrich the lives of the elderly. The suggestions outlined here will show you new ways to communicate.

We all know how to talk – we learned that before we walked. Yet, listening is truly an art. Most of us have heard about it; few practice it well. Real listening says to a person, "You are important to me." Elderly residents do not have many close relatives or friends to talk to. It is particularly important for them to have the opportunity to really talk and have someone really listen. It makes them feel good, their self-esteem gets a boost, they may have pleasant thoughts after you leave that will linger for a long time. What counts, when communicating with your elderly relative, is the richness of contact and the meaningfulness of the content. The following pages are designed with suggestions to accomplish just that.

WHAT TO TALK ABOUT

When you go to visit your elderly relative, talk about the family, the children, grandchildren, siblings. Don't be afraid to share "bad news" as well as "good." Elderly residents have lived through much sadness, pain and death. Protecting them usually makes them feel cheated and left out. Share the joys and the sorrows; they have a right to know. For a change try not starting your conversation with "how are you today?" Instead show the elderly person that you remembered what they said last time you visited. Try not to talk about the weather, it's a boring topic. If you have difficulty finding things to talk about, try these:

Current events in outside life, the neighborhood, new neighbors;

Family;

Seasonal changes, for example: the birds at your feeder, what's in the garden this week;

Sporting events;

Concerts, plays, etc.;

Service groups or clubs they used to attend. They may still be able to go to some meetings or to the annual banquet; if they can't, tell them about the luncheon, the guest speaker, who wore what, etc.;

Special interests: sewing, weaving, stamp collecting, making models, music;

Pets;

Church services you've attended;

Careers;

Trips;

The "old" days;

Their home;

Their "Home";

TV or radio programs.

PAST TALK – REMINISCING

There are two very important words in the English language which you and I use more frequently than we realize. One could simply not manage without them at a high school reunion. These two words become increasingly meaningful as we get older and are extremely important to the elderly. They are – Remember When . . .

- we stole all the carrots out of Mrs. Parsons garden . . .
- the boys and girls lined up on either side of the gym during the junior prom – and the crinolines . . .
- we used to bake bread together and put it by the hot air register to rise . . .
- the great fire, (flood, earthquake) hit.

"Remember whens" could go on for a hundred years – in fact they do go on for as long as we live – that's why there are so many to listen to. Present life for too many elderly institutionalized people is often dull. Their reservoir of memories is a colorful addition to a bleak present.

The Same Old Story: Listening to the same old story over and over again can be very tiring and test even the most patient person. There may be good reason why certain stories get repeated so often. As you listen to the content, understand the feelings, feel the mood. What was so happy or sad or important about what the other person is expressing? As recent memory fails long-ago events may gain more detail each time they are relived.

Like you and me, older persons want to feel good about themselves. One of the ways they can do that is to tell about the times when they felt important and had significant experiences. They may have been an important sports figure, invented something, raised fourteen children (or was it sixteen?). These events from the past can be related to present day situations and add special meaning to the elderly person's present existence.

> *Listening is a magnetic and strange thing, a creative force. The friends who listen to us are the ones we move toward, and we want to sit in their radius. When we are listened to, it creates us, makes us unfold and expand.* – Karl Menninger

We need to listen to the stories again and again. They have been engraved on the memory of the elderly. They may be delightful renderings of childhood. "When I was a young girl, I walked to school along a country road, across the wheat fields. I used to hear the wolves yowl in the nearby woods and my footsteps would begin to . . ."

You may feel like screaming inside when your elderly relative begins a worn-out tale, but try to learn something new about the person. How did she feel when she heard the wolves – courageous? afraid? Is she telling you how tough times were and how well she handled it – does she want some recognition for this? Ask about details of the story and don't be surprised that the facts get embellished. One day she might even borrow her brother's rifle to shoot the wolves. And it helps to remember that the best gauge for knowing and understanding the elderly person is what they tell us about themselves.

Often reminiscing creates an opportunity to finish any unfinished business. You won't be able to after they have died. Tell them you're sorry about . . . or glad about . . . tell them you love them, tell them you remember when they did . . . for you.

Reminiscing can be:

- entertaining, when humorous stories from the past are shared;
- a way of exchanging information that can be surprising and inspiring;
- a way of problem-solving through giving suggestions and encouragement;
- educational when historic information is shared.

Life Review: So You Were A Milkman: Reminiscing has been described as "living in a memory." Experts tell us that reminiscing about past experiences may be a way of coping or adapting to present situations. Exploring and evaluating the elderly's earlier life, coming to terms with previous disappointments and failures, enjoying past successes and pleasures and resolving conflicts is a main developmental task in later life and helps the elderly person to achieve peace of mind.

Inherent in reviewing our lives through reminiscing is the consideration of the sorrows and pain of life as well as the joys. They both need to be considered and put into perspective. Clearly for some the reminiscing experience is painful. However, many elderly view reminiscing in positive terms and derive satisfaction from the ability to find peace of mind as they reflect, evaluate and resolve minor and major events. Life review work could help alleviate communication difficulties between you and your elderly relative, making your time together more productive and meaningful.

Experts suggest that the purpose of reminiscence is to maintain self-esteem, to stimulate thinking and to enhance a natural healing process that comes with life review, so that older people can find meaning, worth and an acceptance of what life has been.

Here are some suggestions for helping your elderly relative review their life through reminiscing:

- Go through the old photograph albums;
- Talk about the family, library books, crafts, hobbies, war medals and certificates for achievement;
- Read poetry and the lyrics of songs;
- Discuss past careers. Find out, for example, what it was like to be a milkman in the 40's and 50's and how that has changed;
- Relate past events to the present situation, thereby establishing continuity and helping to make some sense and meaning out of life;
- Talk and ask about how things began, for example, do they remember the Box Camera?

Sample Questions for Reviewing Life

1. Where were you born? What was it like to live there? How did you handle difficult times?
2. What were your parents like, your siblings, other relatives?
3. What hobbies and activities did you do as a young person?
4. Did you enjoy your working life?
5. How many different jobs did you have? Tell me about them.
6. What do you think are the best years of your life?
7. How would you describe your attitude toward life?

Music: A Vehicle for Reviewing the Past

> *Music produces a kind of pleasure which human nature cannot do without.* – Confucius

Music is a powerful vehicle for reviewing one's life. Often it happens almost unconsciously when we hear an old song that pulls us back to a previous era – a time when we danced the jitterbug, the jive, or enjoyed a family sing-along. Remember when we'd crank up the phonograph and listen to "Don't Sit Under the Apple Tree?" The lyrics were pretty easy, remember – "Don't sit under the apple tree, with anyone else but me. Anyone else but me. Anyone else but me. No, no, no. Don't sit . . . under . . . the . . . ap . . . . . .ple . . . . tree . . . . with" and as the song ground to a halt you'd grab the handle and furiously wind-up to hear the last line – "anybody else but me. Anybodyelsebutme..." – in quadruple time. Ah, those were the good old days – or were they? For often, reminiscing and reviewing life through music can be a very painful experience. Claribel put it much better than I can:

I Cannot Sing the Old Songs
I sang long years ago,
For heart and voice would fail me
And foolish tears would flow
For by-gone hours come o'er my heart
With each familiar strain:
I Cannot Sing the Old Songs
Or dream those dreams again.

Music is very closely linked to the stages of our life – from childhood, to adulthood and finally to old age. These stages could be likened to the bar lines in a piece of music – they do serve to help us "count our time" or number our days – but if the bars are removed, the music is freed and moves smoothly from one great event to another. From conception to our death and beyond the grave could be the total life span. Life has cycles, rhythm, joy and pain, as does music. Music creates an essential structure with a beginning, a middle and an end, enabling us to explore all aspects of life, all the separate parts, in an integrated whole. Combine the power of music and its structure with the events of our lives and a trigger will be released, a trigger that can stimulate our inner most being and assist us in living in a memory.

Melody exists in the soul of man. The soul is indeed the harp upon which the musician plays. – Rudolph Steiner

Music serves every part of us – the social, physical, intellectual and emotional. Memories of the past that are associated with music are, fortunately, usually pleasant. Lullabies, songs of childhood, hymns, school choruses and even war songs have happy associations and give music its power to socialize. Through the musical experience we aim at intellectual stimulation and emotional comfort as we take a musical journey through life.

Tell me the tales that to me were so dear
Sing me the songs I delighted to hear....
Let me believe that you love as you lov'd
Long, Long Ago, Long Ago.
– T.H. Bagley

Sample Questions to ask for Reviewing Life through Music

1. When was the first time you heard this song?
2. Who sang it?
3. What was happening in your life at this time?
4. How do you feel about the song now?
5. Does it still affect you the same way as it did when you first heard it?
6. What are your favorite songs? Why do you like them? Would you like me to sing (play) them for you?

FUTURE TALK

One of the things we often neglect when talking to the elderly is the future. They do have one, even if it isn't likely to be as long as yours and mine. An important question that many elderly ask of themselves is, "Who can I be?" It is, therefore, extremely important for you to be involved in their future. You have been part of the past, you are with them in the present, and talk of the future gives a sense of security and comfort. Here are some topics for future talk:

- Residents' council;
- Community Services: stuffing envelopes or giving a "talk" to a group of students are ways to contribute;
- Outings;
- Helping other residents;
- New interests;
- Continued involvement in service clubs or organizations;
- Upcoming major family events: anniversaries, birthdays, weddings.

Talking about Dying

> *What makes old age so sad is not that our joys but our hopes cease.* – Jean Paul Richter

An old person may want to talk about dying. This is an important topic for elderly residents who have lived a long life and who are tired of coping with the inevitable losses that come with old age. They may indicate their desire to die by saying "I'm just so tired of living" or they may try to tell you that they don't want their life prolonged when the time comes for emergency measures. A "living will" signed by the elderly person gives guidance to the physicians and family to withhold life-sustaining equipment and medication in the event they are no longer able to say this for themselves.

Some elderly persons openly express a wish to end their lives. Some succeed in doing so. Hearing this from an elderly loved one conjures up complicated feelings of how to help the elderly person particularly when we might agree that death at some point is better than the present quality of life. Talking about these profound issues is necessary and may be much more helpful to the elderly person than *anything* else you can do or say.

We need to recognize the topic of death and dying when it begins to surface in subtle ways. We need to share feelings and give permission to the old person (and to ourselves) to talk, to weep and to feel. We need at times to display some courage to help our loved ones to finish their lives. We need to start thinking about these important issues of life now, so that we are more comfortable discussing them when it is appropriate. One of the ways to introduce the topic of dying is by talking about someone else. For example, you could say, "Mrs. Smith wanted to be cremated," or "at Mr. Brown's funeral we sang the beautiful hymn, *Rock of Ages*. What are your favorite hymns?" "When I die I'm going to have a funeral service. What would you prefer, a memorial service or funeral service?"

PRESENT TALK – HOW TO TALK ABOUT IT

> *That is the happiest conversation where there is no competition, no vanity, but a calm quiet interchange of sentiments.* – Samuel Johnson

Communication Skills

Check it out.

Paraphrase or summarize in your own words what the elderly person has said. Ask if the person thinks you've understood them. This shows that you are really listening.

"Own" your message.

By using the word "I" you take ownership of what you say: "I feel annoyed when you ... ," instead of "you make me annoyed when you ..."

Acknowledge Feelings.

This makes the other person feel understood: "Are you feeling sad because your budgie bird died?"

Negative Forms of Communication

Teasing: An attempt to provoke anger, resentment or confusion.

Patronizing: Don't "talk down" as if elderly were children.

Names: "Dearie" may be an inappropriate term of endearment for some elderly; if you don't know the person well ask them what they would prefer to be called.

Gossip: Don't!

Sarcasm: A comment, when angry, designed to cut or give pain; one of the "lowest" forms of communication.

INGREDIENTS FOR MEANINGFUL COMMUNICATION

For Talking

Remove roadblocks.

- Minimize distractions as much as possible;
- Arrange seating. Don't scatter a number of visitors around the room; this makes it difficult for many elderly to concentrate on the conversation;
- Establish eye contact;
- Sit face-to-face;
- Avoid giving directions, it can create dependence;
- Don't "talk down."

Be clear and make yourself understood.

- Avoid long cumbersome sentences or words;

- Don't make assumptions that the elderly person understands everything you are saying;
- Use a pleasant tone of voice;
- Don't talk too fast.

Give elderly people "the benefit of the doubt."

Try to avoid unpleasant arguments.

Ask open-ended questions, not questions that can only be answered by "yes," or "no."

This technique allows the other person more freedom, encourages conversation and indicates that you are interested in what is being said. For example: "What was shown at the slide presentation?", instead of, "Did you enjoy the slide presentation?" (yes/no)

After you have been talking to your relative you have a right to a response from them if they are able.

If at times you don't get one you may need to repeat what you have said as the elderly person may not have heard you, may not have understood you, is not feeling well, is tuning you out, is choosing not to respond, or is taking time out as a hearing impaired person may do. You may need to be quite direct about asking for a response. However, there is likely a very good reason and you may need to get a professional staff member to help you.

Listening is Worth Talking About

> *Two men were walking along a crowded sidewalk in a downtown business area. Suddenly one exclaimed: "Listen to the lovely sound of that cricket." But the other could not hear. He asked his companion how he could detect the sound of a cricket amid the din of people and traffic. The first man, a zoologist, had trained himself to listen to the voices of nature. But he didn't explain. He simply took a coin out of his pocket and dropped it to the sidewalk, whereupon a dozen people began to look about for it. "We hear," he said, "what we listen for."*
>
> – Kermit L. Long

Listening is a skill that must be learned – it is not just a matter of keeping quiet. It involves heavy use of our two ears and minimal use of our one tongue. The word listen is defined as "to hear something with thoughtful attention."

Listen with your EARS.
Listen with your EYES.
Listen with your HEART.

Listening Skills

Listening is a million dollar gift that costs you nothing.

1. Stop talking.
2. Show that you're interested and want to listen: Sit down and get comfortable. Give your full attention. Your body posture and the expression on your face indicate if you're interested. Consider their needs and interests.
3. Respond when appropriate: Don't interrupt with a similar story. Try to "catch" the person saying something positive and focus the conversation on that. You don't have to agree or disagree if you are trying to see the other person's point of view. Listen to understand, not just to reply.
4. Be empathetic: Try to picture the world as the elderly person sees it. Have you ever sat in a wheelchair?
5. Be aware of the physical needs – hearing, seeing, touching – position yourself at a comfortable distance.
6. Listen to content and to feelings. What is the person trying to tell you about themselves or their situation? They may have a lot of pent-up feelings and have a right to vent them. It is extremely important to acknowledge other people's feelings and not to deny them.
7. Allow angry feelings. Try not to take offence if the elderly person seems angry or critical. Elderly in care facilities are dependent for many things. This is not just mildly frustrating but is often cause for extreme anger against a situation they cannot control. It is necessary and healthy for an elderly person to ventilate their negative feelings: this may help resolve what is bothering them. When angry feelings turn into abusive attacks on a visiting relative, however, that is a different matter and in extreme cases leads some relatives to stop visiting each other temporarily or altogether.
8. Be patient. Some old people need more time to think and talk; they may respond slowly or repeat themselves: Allow enough time for the full expression of ideas. Remember that the more impor-

tant the idea, the longer it may take to express it. Try not to speed up the conversation by finishing the elderly person's sentence.

9. You may want to avoid focusing on symptoms and treatment. If your elderly relative belabors the topic of ailments, they may be trying to tell you something other than what they are specifically saying. You may want to check with the staff about the problem. It may be something of real concern.

10. Finally, be aware of the resident's personal space. They may not want you sitting on their bed or leaning over them. Quiet visitors or over-talkative visitors are tiring: 50% talk and 50% listen is a good rule of thumb. Five minutes of real contact has real power.

Is patience one of your virtues? If not, here are some tips for becoming more patient:

- Take a break – get away from the situation;
- Seek support – talk it over with someone;
- Ventilate – get your feelings out, allow yourself to be angry;
- Breathe – take a few deep breaths;
- Rest – get plenty of it;
- Count – to 10 or 20 or 120.

We most often associate patience with the need for more of it, as well as being the opposite of hastiness or impetuousness. The word patient also means bearing pains or trials calmly or without complaint. Quite a challenge? True. When all else fails and your patience is running thin, remember: "A handful of patience is worth more than a bushel of brains."

Pleas from the Other Side:

Could You Just Listen?

When I ask you to listen to me and you start giving me advice, you have not done what I asked.

When I ask you to listen to me and you begin to tell me why I shouldn't feel that way, you are trampling on my feelings.

When I ask you to listen to me and you feel you have to do something to solve my problem, you have failed me, strange as that may seem.

Listen! All I asked was that you listen, not talk or do – just hear me.

I can do for myself; I'm not helpless – maybe discouraged and faltering, but not helpless.

When you do something for me that I can and need to do for myself, you contribute to my fear and inadequacy.

But when you accept as a simple fact that I do feel what I feel, no matter how irrational, then I can quit trying to convince you and can get about the business of understanding what's behind this irrational feeling. When that's clear, the answers are obvious and I don't need advice.

Perhaps that's why prayer works, sometimes, for some people – because God is mute, and He/She doesn't give advice or try to fix things. "They" just listen and let you work it out for yourself.

So please listen and just hear me.

And if you want to talk, wait a minute for your turn – and I'll listen to you. – Author Anonymous

Silence Has a Lot to Say

The notes I handle no better than many pianists. But the pauses between the notes - ah, that is where the art resides! – Arthur Schnabel

Silence has a lot to say and there are many ways to express it. Every moment together does not have to be filled with talking. There is no need to be afraid of silence; listen to it, let the world and your mind be still for a moment. Feel the silence – it calms, it soothes, it comforts. Try not to cut in when the other person is *thinking*. Sharing the stillness is communicating.

Silence, for some, is a time of great discomfort. You may wonder why the elderly person does not answer, or may seem to have drifted off miles away. Sometimes you may conjure up images of happy times or sad times – often of times that are no more. An elderly person may revel in "this place," or it might be too emotionally charged to talk about. This is a good time to take advantage of the silence – not by breaking it, but by just "being present."

DO'S AND DON'TS CHECKLIST

Do's

1. Do allow the resident to set the pace.
2. Do look at the resident, preferably at eye level.
3. Do accept silences.
4. Do respond to the feelings that are being expressed.
5. Do state your feelings from time to time.
6. Do use your sense of humor and be yourself.
7. Do sit down and get comfortably settled.
8. Do give your message clearly and slowly.
9. Do act in a friendly, non-critical manner.
10. Do remember the positive things about the resident.

Don'ts

1. Don't take things too personally.
2. Don't stand towering over the bed or chair.
3. Don't try to solve all the resident's problems.
4. Don't use an interview style, asking too many questions.
5. Don't busy yourself with daily tasks in place of meaningful conversation.
6. Don't bounce up and down on the resident's bed if you get angry.
7. Don't give advice unless it's asked for.
8. Don't say "Everyone feels that way."
9. Don't say "Are you ever lucky to be in here, being waited on; I wish I could spend a few days here" or "I wish I could trade you places for a day or two."
10. Don't give up trying to improve communication.

Touch: Touch has a language of its own. Touching is the most important non-verbal means of communication for the elderly. A pat on the head can be patronizing, but a handshake with special warmth, a touch on the shoulder, holding hands, touching the face, brushing hair, rubbing fingers, massaging hands or a warm hug helps to reduce stress and aches and pains. This brings comfort and generally makes the elderly person feel cared about. Love often needs no words and what will really be remembered is the touching.

Cents of Humor: At Whose Expense

> *The real wit tells jokes to make others feel superior, while the half-wit tells them to make others feel small.* – Elmer Wheeler

Humor is an important part of communication. Unfortunately, we often omit it from our conversations, thinking that to jest is foolish or stupid. "Fools" in the past were kept in great households to provide casual entertainment and to amuse royalty. Today we can see a comedy movie – fun for the moment, but what about the other 22 hours of the day? A sense of humor is not an overly cheery attitude that attempts to cover up problems – "Oh, things could be worse." False cheerfulness can make some people feel worse.

Humor is something designed to be comical or amusing and when it results in genuine laughter you know you have hit the mark. Using your sense of humor can help people simply feel better all over. Laughter is a great way to release tiredness and aches and pains of the body and mind. How refreshed we feel around the bubbly person who tells a good joke or punsters with their effervescent attitude – even groaning at them feels good.

Humor, when used appropriately, is one of the best medicines money can buy. It can raise the spirit and sense of well-being of almost anyone. Life is not very funny for most institutionalized elderly. It is difficult to find things to really have a good laugh about. Having a sense of humor allows us to see the fun and lightens our daily experiences. Teasing, or making jokes at someone else's expense, on the other hand, is not usually funny. It's more effective to make a joke on yourself than on others. Bring a joke book to share or get a funny movie for all the residents to watch. Bring in funny pictures of the kids "acting-up." If you can get your elderly relative to really laugh you will have made the visit and the next long week for them happier and more enjoyable.

HOW AND WHEN TO TALK TO PROFESSIONALS

Tact is the art of making your point without making an enemy.
– Howard W. Newton

The Staff: It is vitally important to develop and maintain a good relationship with staff members in the Nursing Home. When visiting, relatives and staff work together towards the common goal of providing the best possible care, the elderly resident is the ultimate beneficiary. The relationship between both groups needs to be one of mutual trust and understanding and above all one in which good communication flows smoothly.

It is a good idea for one main visitor to have contact with the staff. When too many relatives get involved the issues and concerns become unnecessarily complicated. It is important to exchange information with staff on an on-going basis, therefore co-operation on both sides is crucial. Be considerate of the staff. You do not always know the full circumstances in any given situation. Attempt to find out the facts if something seems wrong to you. What may seem like a major problem to you, may not be to the staff. However, you are entitled to expect quality care for your relative. One of the best ways of getting it is to communicate effectively with all of the staff in the Home.

How to Annoy a Staff Member:

- Make demands at the busy times such as meal or bath times;
- Complain about small details instead of asking what you can do to help;
- Never express your appreciation for all that they do;
- Take out your frustrations on them;

Unhappy staff are like any other unhappy people and may even give unhappy care. Try to treat them as you would like to be treated.

Guidelines for Problem-Solving

If a problem arises regarding the care of your elderly relative and you need to take action, try these:

1. Listen to the complaints/concerns that are being voiced by your elderly relative;

2. Remain calm, cool and collected;
3. Gather information about the situation – deal with the facts, not just what someone else said;
4. Determine acceptable outcomes: know your expectations and what you hope will result;
5. Identify the person(s) who can take action;
6. Plan a time and a place to meet with the staff;
7. Communicate your point of view and your feelings, and have eye contact when you do this;
8. Give some positive feedback for whatever has been done well;
9. Go to the person higher up the line of authority if necessary;
10. Work together toward a solution;
11. Set a time to review the problem if it has not been resolved;
12. Compromising does not always solve a problem.

Lines of Authority/Chain of Command

The structure of the staff in a care facility is usually as follows. Titles for the various positions may be different. Many facilities have social workers who are available to help you.

- Administrator/Owner
- Director of Nursing/Resident Care
- Registered Nurse
- Care Aide

Often, today we defer or act in a submissive, fearful or unassertive way when we ask for something. This attitude is not necessary when making requests of nursing home staff and furthermore is self-degrading. You have a right to receive appropriate explanations and responses to your questions. Most of us ask questions out of caring. If you sense you are getting the "run-around" from a staff member, go to another staff member or talk to the person who is one step up the chain of command. It might help to remember whose turf we're on. It is your elderly relative's Home, is it not?

The Physician: A difficulty encountered by many visitors is communicating with their elderly relative's doctor. One visitor described the problem this way:

"I was visiting my mother last Sunday and she was in such pain that she said she was going to ask the nurse to phone the doctor. Apparently the nurse had already phoned but the doctor had said he'd see her in four days. I've gone through terrible problems with my back and have experienced and understand excruciating pain. I interfered once and was told by the doctor to mind my own business. So I hate to interfere. If I have anything to say I usually talk to the nurse. We communicate, and that's very important. My mother has been like this now since her last fall over a week ago and except for being given pain-killers nothing is being done. I don't know if anything can be done except perhaps bed rest. I said to my mother, 'One of the reasons it takes so long for it to heal is because you're not as mobile as you used to be and your muscles are not as strong.' She seems to understand that. The most difficult part of visiting for me is the helpless feeling I have. For example, she told me today, 'The doctor will probably tell me to have an X-ray taken, but how am I going to get there?' I couldn't take my mother because I was working the next day and she cannot get in and out of the car. The last time she went for X-rays they took her in an ambulance. It really is a helpless feeling, not knowing what to do. If I could communicate with my mother's doctor that would help immensely."

If you are not confident of the doctor's treatment of your elderly relative's condition or you have difficulty communicating with him or her there are ways to improve the situation. One option, that is often not utilized enough, is changing doctors. This can be as simple as a phone call to have medical records forwarded to a new office.

A major problem can occur, however, if your elderly relative does not want to change doctors and you do not communicate well with the present one. The elderly person may see no need to change doctors or is unaware of the problems you experience. All too often an unhealthy situation is tolerated for months and years because individuals do not take action or do not know how or what to do. You and your elderly relative are entitled to the best possible medical care. If, after discussing the situation, your elderly relative still does not want to change doctors, then you may have to change yourself. Whether you are able to change doctors or change the situation, the rest of this section offers some suggestions.

Finding the Right Doctor[1]

An ongoing, comfortable relationship with a physician you can trust is important, and choosing that particular individual is a highly personal decision. After all, the doctor that's right for one person may not suit another. The better the doctor knows your elderly relative's background and medical history, the easier it is to provide effective long-term treatment.

Start by asking questions – of friends, relatives, acquaintances. Ask which doctors they see, if they are satisfied with their care and what is the doctor's treatment and philosophy.

Hints for Effective Communication with the Doctor

Carry a written list of names and doses of all your relative's prescription medications. Remember to update the list regularly.

Keep a record of all your relative's vaccinations.

Ask questions. It's a good idea to write down any questions you want to ask the doctor before your visit. And it's just as useful to write down the answers, especially if they involve specific instructions. If you don't fully understand what the doctor has told you, ask for clarification. Remember, the doctor wants the advice to help you, and you must understand it before you can follow it.

If you want more information about the condition or problem, ask the doctor to recommend some reading material.

Help your relative follow the doctor's instructions precisely.

If your relative doesn't get better or develops a problem from a treatment, or is unhappy or uncomfortable with it, let the doctor know so an alternate course of action can be taken.

If you are not confident with the doctor's assessment or treatment of your relative's condition get a second opinion.

What should I expect from the doctor?

Some people are content with any doctor. Others have superhuman expectations impossible for anyone to achieve.

Look for a doctor who is:

Competent. All doctors must go through years of specialized study and training in order to be licensed to practise medicine. You should feel confident that the doctor is knowledgeable.

Attentive. Some doctors are better communicators than others. You should be satisfied that the doctor listens and considers what you have to say.

Reasonable. Doctors are all well-versed in the complex, technical, multisyllabic language of medicine, but unless you, too, are a doctor or other health professional, the doctor should not expect you to understand medicalese. He or she should speak to you at your level of understanding.

Explanatory. Finally, the doctor should be a good teacher and explain his or her assessment of your relative's health, any testing required and the plan of treatment.

(In case you didn't notice, all these qualities add up to CARE – the most important attribute to look for in a doctor.)

What does my doctor need to know from me?

Most people visit the doctor for a specific problem. When this is the case, it's best to focus on that problem alone and give an accurate representation of it. Your relative's answers to the following questions will provide the doctor with the necessary information:

What provokes the problem – what brings it on or makes it worse? What prevents it – what makes it go away or relieves it?

Describe the quality and quantity of the symptom. Is it a dull ache that's lasted for a long time or an intermittent, stabbing pain?

On what region of your body is the symptom located? Does it radiate – does it move to other areas of the body or stay in one place?

How severe is the problem? How and when does it interfere with day-to-day life?

What is the timing of the problem – when did it begin, is it constant, does it come and go?

Are there any associated symptoms or other problems that seem to accompany this one?

Giving the doctor this information will save you both a lot of time. More importantly, asking the questions will increase your awareness of your own role in improving and maintaining your relative's health.

7
Special Types of Communication

If you read nothing else in this chapter, please read at least this and the next section. Your relative may be vision, hearing or speech impaired, but please don't skip to the suggestions on a specific impairment. The next section is for everyone. The following pages contain a myriad of ways to improve communication, but learning new and effective techniques for communication is only part of the process. Another critical factor is attitude.

ATTITUDE MAKES THE WORLD DIFFERENT

Society's attitude toward impaired or handicapped persons is still in the Dark Ages and is perhaps the biggest problem inherent in any impairment. Individuals still treat the handicapped as second, third or fourth class citizens. This negative attitude creates an almost impossible situation for the impaired person who has little or no control over it.

A deaf person can learn to read lips, a blind person can learn to navigate and to perform daily tasks. But, what skill can an elderly person learn to change a negative attitude? I haven't been able to discover any. Certainly, impaired people can take some responsibility for asking individuals to help them. But put yourself in the position of always needing to ask for help. What would you rather be; the helper or the helpee? Which position is viewed as the one of independence and strength?

Those of us who have lived with an impaired spouse, parent, sibling or child are often well-equipped with skills to communicate effectively and develop a proper attitude toward the disability. Not all family members fall into this category: some may withdraw in various ways from the impaired person or they may give up early and never really implement the necessary skills. Often friends or other relatives are keenly aware of communication difficulties, but it doesn't necessarily follow that they do anything to communicate more effectively. Many people do try but give up in frustration. They may simply lack the patience required to have any sort of meaningful contact with an impaired person. Some factors to keep in mind are:

- The handicapped person wants to understand you;
- They must accept their part in the communication process (they often don't for various reasons);
- You have a wide variety of techniques to help the person understand: written notes, chalkboards, help from others including staff.

Those of us who live or who have lived with an impaired person are in a position to educate others about the facts of life for a handicapped person. If each of us resolved to teaching five people a year for a number of years we might make some inroads that would begin to eradicate the harmful attitude. This teaching could emphasize:

- recognizing that impaired people are like you and me on the inside and treating them as such;
- learning patience – you'll need lots;
- making allowances for the disability but not over-compensating for it;
- showing respect by not doing everything for them;
- learning communication techniques that will decrease misunderstanding and help to prevent suspicion and distrust.

Consider the elderly person who is visually or hearing impaired, maybe a little of both. Add to that the pain of arthritis or some other chronic problem and you have a pile-up of disabilities, which make communication for the elderly person extraordinarily difficult.

One thing is certain, you can find a way to communicate with impaired people. It takes caring, creativity, imagination, tenacity, patience and confidence. It takes going the extra mile (sometimes an inch will do), it takes not giving up. A difficult combination of personal characteristics? Maybe. Challenging and exhausting? Yes. But the end result – an elderly impaired person feeling a part of the world – makes it all worth while.

Communicating with the hearing and speech impaired involves great difficulties for both the handicapped person and family member.

Therefore these topics are dealt with at length in this chapter. Sections on visual impairment and wheelchair etiquette have been included, although their needs are not entirely restricted to communication concerns but relate more to the tasks of daily living.

THE HEARING IMPAIRED

If you have skipped to this point before reading the section entitled "Attitude Makes the World Different," you will have missed the essence of my message. Please go back and read it now.

The Invisible Handicap[1]

Hearing impairment, unlike many physical handicaps, may go unnoticed even when an individual is wearing a hearing aid. As a result, the general public may be insensitive to the difficulties of hearing impaired people. Hearing loss in an elderly person may have many detrimental effects. She or he may withdraw from the family and from other social situations. Many persons cease communicating because of an inability to hear and understand what others are saying.

What should be done? If your elderly relative experiences difficulty in hearing they should see a physician, preferably an otolaryngologist (Ear & Throat doctor) to determine if medical treatment is necessary. If a physician cannot solve the problem medically, then they must see an audiologist, who will test their hearing to determine if a hearing aid can help. The audiologist will select the appropriate type of amplification to help make speech louder and more understandable. An audiologist is a university-trained professional with a Master's degree in audiology, which is the study of hearing, auditory assessment, hearing aids and rehabilitation.

Physicians have, in the past, often told patients that a hearing aid will not help an age-related hearing loss. However, hearing aids have improved significantly in recent years and most individuals with this type of loss do benefit from hearing aid use. Other devices have also been developed for specific environmental sounds such as the phone, TV, the doorbell, and fire alarms. An audiologist will help to identify which of these devices might be useful to the elderly person.

> *Hearing Aids:* Very few people can put on a hearing aid and hear comfortably right away. Hearing aids make sounds louder; they do not correct hearing. Learning to listen with a hearing aid is an important part of the aural rehabilitation process. Professional instruction in learning to listen is called auditory training. A period of instruction and practice can mean years of better hearing.

A hearing aid is not necessarily the solution to hearing loss. Older persons often dislike wearing them. Adjusting to a hearing aid can be difficult and frustrating and ultimately may not improve hearing. It is extremely important to be patient with a hard-of-hearing person. Special provisions are made in many places for handicapped people in general, but seldom are there any provisions made for those with hearing loss.

Paying Lipservice to a Lipreader Lipreading or speechreading involves an impaired person watching the speaker's face to help supplement hearing. It is the ability to understand spoken language without fully hearing or without hearing at all. Most of us do it naturally without realizing that we are doing it. The hearing impaired person, on the other hand, must learn this skill in order to communicate. There are many suggestions in this chapter to assist the impaired person to hear.

I have never read that "touching improves hearing," but it does, and it has nothing to do with physiology. It has everything to do with a caring attitude. When we care, we get close and we touch. This, like nothing else, tells the deaf person "I care enough about you and the conversation we're about to have that I'm going to do everything I can to enable you to hear me." Paying lipservice to a lipreader will never aid communication. Knowing what to do is not enough. We must do it. Actions speak as loud as words.

Have You Ever Tried Lipreading? This section has been included to give some idea of what you and the person lipreading need to be aware of for greater understanding of the disability. It is a list of practical suggestions for lipreaders. You have permission to photocopy this page. Give it to the hearing impaired person to read and then discuss it together. When both parties take a share of responsibility for communication you will be amazed what a deaf person can hear.

Suggestions for Lipreaders[2]

1. Have the light at your back.
2. Stand far enough back to see the speaker's face.
3. Be willing to ask people to repeat.
4. Be sure that the other person is not embarrassed by your inability to hear. Move away from background noise such as air conditioners, music, crowded rooms.
5. Don't attempt to bluff. It's better to admit your hearing loss and work from there. Ask others to speak slowly and clearly. Remind the speaker not to cover their lips.
6. Keep sociable. Cultivate your friends.
7. Have a wide variety of interests, and keep abreast of what is going on in the world so you can contribute to conversations.
8. Explain, if necessary, that the aid does not give you normal hearing and that you would appreciate having the speaker face you, talk clearly, and not shout.
9. Get enough rest. At all times there is a certain amount of nervous strain on the speech reader, and since one cannot concentrate fully when tired and nervous, an extra amount of relaxation is necessary in order to be alert when attending to speech.
10. Use your imagination. If you "get" only one of several words, you may often be able to guess what the other words are, or at least get the meaning, if you stop and think about it. Lip formation, facial expressions, imagination and intuition all figure in speech interpretation.

Do not be discouraged. Learning speech reading takes time and practice. Even some of the experts have "blank" spells when they cannot read speech any better than a novice does. You are not the only one who has an occasional mental block. If you encounter difficulty in speechreading, try to figure out why. Look at the situation, the speaker, etc., before blaming yourself.

Some Common Misconceptions About Deafness[3]

"Deaf Persons Can Read Lips"

Speechreading or lipreading is a skill that some deaf persons are good at; others have difficulty mastering such a talent. While good speechreading skill can help in communication, only part of speech is visible on the lips, and even the best speechreaders can't speechread everything that is said.

"Deaf Persons Are Not Distracted When They Work In A Noisy Environment"

Most deaf persons have some residual hearing, and if they wear hearing aids they may be even more sensitive to sounds and vibrations than most hearing persons.

"People Who Have Unusual Sounding Speech Are Mentally Impaired"

There is absolutely no correlation between a deaf person's speech and intelligence.

"Deaf Persons Don't Use the Telephone"

Some deaf persons have enough residual hearing and have developed the speech skills necessary to use the telephone. Special telecommunication aids have been developed for hard of hearing and deaf people.

"Deaf Persons' Speech is Difficult to Understand"

The speech intelligibility of deaf persons varies greatly from one deaf person to another. Many deaf persons have speech that seems difficult to understand at first, but after spending some time with these persons, their speech becomes easier to understand.

What is it Really Like to be Deaf/Hard of Hearing? No one can know what it is really like to be hard of hearing. We can plug our ears with cotton balls to smother sound, or turn the radio just slightly off the station. The fact is we can always correct the error. There are, however, a few effective ways of experiencing the enormous frustrations lived through by most deaf people. Experiencing an impairment is the quickest way to develop the skills needed to communicate more effectively with a hard of hearing person.

Here are two exercises that will allow you to get into the shoes of a hard of hearing person. In order for your "inner heart" to really get the message you'll have to take time out from your busy schedule.

Exercise No. 1:

First of all you will need to set aside a half day for this exercise. Then you will need to locate in the phone book a community center or multi-cultural center that offers activities to people in a language other than your own. Call them up and ask to join one of the discussion groups for one afternoon session. Make sure that no one in the group speaks English. Be in the group for the whole afternoon, at least two to three hours. Take part in the social time.

Take note of how certain individuals treat you, especially the ones who are resentful of you, the ones that can't be bothered with you. Make the exercise work for you – it can easily be done and will do wonders for attuning your empathy. How did you feel during the afternoon? What new awareness do you have?

Exercise No. 2:

This exercise is convenient and easy to do, can be done right in your own home and only takes one hour, that is, if you can last that long. Pick your favorite TV program, sit down as usual to watch it – with the sound completely off. That night for one hour watch your favorite program in silence. Really watch. Look at the gestures, what are they really saying to each other, why did he do that? After the hour is up – you are going to stick it out for the hour aren't you? – ask yourself how you felt, what you learned or become aware of, etc.

Communicating with a Hard of Hearing Person[4,5]

1. Look directly at the person while speaking. Even a slight turn of the head can obscure the deaf person's vision. Other distracting factors affecting communication include moustaches obscuring the lips and habits such as smoking, pencil-chewing, and putting hands in front of the face.

2. Speak slowly and clearly, but don't exaggerate or overemphasize words. This distorts lip movements, making speechreading more difficult.

3. It is important to have the deaf person's attention before speaking. Since deaf people can't hear the usual call to attention, they may need a tap on the shoulder, a wave of the hand, or other visual signals to gain attention.

4. Pantomime, body language and facial expression are important factors in communication. Be sure you use all of them.

5. Try to maintain eye contact with the deaf person. Eye contact helps convey the feeling of direct communication. If an interpreter is present, continue to talk directly to the deaf person, who can turn to the interpreter if the need arises.

6. Try to rephrase a thought rather than repeating the same words. Sometimes a group of lip movements is difficult to speechread. If the person doesn't understand you, try to restate the sentence.

7. Don't be embarrassed about communicating via paper and pencil. Getting the message across is more important than the medium.

8. In communicating with a deaf person it is a good idea to remember that intelligence, personality, age at onset of deafness, language background, listening skills, lipreading and speech abilities all vary with each deaf person, just as the skills and personality of each person vary.

9. Every deaf person will communicate in a different way. Some will use speech only; some will use a combination of sign language, fingerspelling and speech; some will write; some will use body language and facial expressions to supplement their interactions. In any case a deaf person will use every possible way to convey an idea to another person.

10. The hearing impaired person's understanding of conversation is partly your responsibility.

11. Most hearing problems do not benefit from loudness so it doesn't help to shout to someone wearing a hearing aid.

12. Other people's accents are a problem for the hearing impaired person. If you have an accent, be ready to use a pen and paper.

13. At parties or meetings, don't limit the conversations to essentials or niceties. It can be frustrating for a person to be without the chance to join in.

14. Accusations that the hard-of-hearing person "hears only what he wants to" are unjust. In order to pick up information, he has to concentrate harder and tires easily. So, in actuality, he does hear "only what he can." When he is tired or distracted or ill, he is less able to hear and understand. His ability to hear changes with each situation.

15. Impatience with his listening behavior will not help; it will only cause him to tense up and hear less. The more relaxed and accepted the hard-of-hearing person feels, the more he can communicate.

16. Find out if he has a "good" ear. Speak to that side.

17. A "deadpan" face is difficult. Remember that the tone of voice may not be heard so use all your acting powers to help project the meaning.

18. Hearing aids do not restore 100% hearing. They amplify sound and increase the distance at which the wearer can hear it, but they cannot restore lost frequencies. Be prepared for confusions and help your friend to laugh at them.

19. Hearing loss need not mean loss of fun. Theatre, music, dancing can all, with a little forethought, still be part of their life.

20. Loss can bring loneliness to the hard of hearing. Too often they begin to feel isolated. Too often others stop talking to them or feel embarrassed with them, simply because they don't know how to "get through." A little informed courtesy can make the loss seem less.

[Adapted from "The Hearing Impaired Patient," courtesy of the Canadian Hearing Society.]

Additional Tips:

- Be aware of possible emotional responses such as: embarrassment, denial, anger, withdrawal, frustration, disorientation, confusion.
- Begin every conversation by positioning yourself close to and in front of the hard-of-hearing person. This will help them relax and know that you care by the effort you're making.
- If you are not being understood, ask the person what you can do differently.
- From time to time ask the person how well you are doing. They often respond with a positive comment that will make you feel appreciated for your effort.
- A pad of paper and pencil are often necessary for writing down key words or phrases. Be aware, however, of the elderly person who can't read; they may be too embarrassed to tell you.
- Candlelight dinners are not a treat for a deaf person who can't see your face. They need to see your face to facilitate lipreading. Also they can't eat their food while it's hot if they are watching talk.
- Take time to include the deaf person in a group situation; they feel hurt and frustrated because of missing so much.
- Don't talk to the deaf person's friend just because it is easier. Try several different ways of communicating with a deaf person until you find one or a combination of ways that work.
- Most important of all DON'T GIVE UP. If you give up on communicating, you give up on the person.

In the Case of Hospitalization

- Put a notice on the hospital chart and above the patients' bed.
- Remember – the hearing impaired person can't lipread through curtains or in the dark.
- Make chaplains or volunteer visitors aware of the hearing impairment.
- Don't do anything unexpected from behind.
- Tap the mattress to get the patient's attention if his/her back is turned.

- Don't restrict a patient's hands, in case he uses sign language.
- Don't leave the patient in complete darkness; leave a dim light on.
- Make sure the hearing aid is within easy reach.

THE VISUALLY IMPAIRED

While they were saying among themselves, "it can't be done," it was done. – Helen Keller

If you haven't read the first section of this chapter entitled "Attitude Makes the World Different," please do so before reading on. Both the visually-impaired and family members or friends have an adjustment to make when they come together. We need to learn and understand what visual impairment is and how it affects your relationship.

Any threatened or actual loss of sight arouses a deep emotional response – usually one of grief, fear and anger.[6] It may be fear of a change in lifestyle, fear of financial dependence and loss of freedom.

A person who becomes visually-impaired or blind through accident or illness may react with resentment, hostility or depression. All of these are normal reactions – and may come suddenly or gradually. Many people become physically disoriented for a time. New thought patterns and new techniques must be developed.

How quickly the person adjusts to loss of sight depends to a large extent on how that person adjusted to life before blindness occurred. Patience and understanding from family and friends as well as discussions with health care professionals can do a great deal to soften the blow and make adjustment easier. However, too much concern or overprotection can hinder the blind person's efforts towards the personal independence necessary for his self-confidence and self-respect.

Most people lose their sight gradually and there is no sudden change in their way of living. In these cases adjustment occurs by degrees. Just remember that a visually-impaired person is a person first and visually-impaired second. Common courtesy and consideration are the basis of any successful relationship.

Ways for Assisting the Blind[7]

1. Identify yourself at once when entering a blind person's room or when meeting a blind neighbor on the street. Approach them from the front rather than the side or back. They may not have recognized your voice. Put the blind person on equal footing. When you are ready to leave, tell them you are leaving.
2. There is no other way to say it. Do not hesitate to use words like "look", "see", "read", nor is there any need to raise your voice.
3. Resist ancient attitudes towards blindness. Treat the blind as any other citizen. Treat the blind person as you would the sighted. Not all blind persons are totally blind; many have some sight.
4. Don't be over-protective. They should do as much as they can for themselves.
5. Always talk directly to a blind person, not through his companion, and use his name. The blind can speak for themselves.
6. When in a blind person's home, leave his belongings where he has put them. If you move them, he may not be able to find them alone.
7. If you must leave a blind person alone in an unfamiliar place, leave him near something he can touch to maintain contact with his environment. It can be uncomfortable standing alone in an open space.
8. When dining with a blind person, tell him what is being served and explain the position of each portion on the plate – "At the top are the peas," or by relating the position of the food to the face of a clock, "Peas at 12 o'clock." When dining in a restaurant, read the menu aloud – complete with prices – and let them order for themselves.
9. Do your part to keep sidewalks clear. Cars jutting across the sidewalk, bikes, skates, garbage cans, etc., can obstruct or injure a blind person.
10. Learn to keep doors all the way closed, or all the way open. Keep drawers closed and chairs pushed in to the table. This makes it easier for the blind or partially sighted person to get around.
11. Refrain from racing your car motor or honking loudly at street crossings. Loud noises can startle or distract the blind person.

12. Do not pat a blind person's guide dog. This distracts the dog and takes his attention away from his duty of guiding his master.
13. Do not grab a blind person's cane in an attempt to lead him.
14. Do not be misinformed. Eyes cannot be weakened or damaged by normal use.
15. Do not be misled. Before deciding a blind person is confused, be sure it is not due to lack of orientation to an area.
16. You may offer to help a blind person locate a bus stop, phone booth, street number, entrance, or other such helpful things. The blind person will tell you "no thanks" if the assistance is not wanted, but it is always nice to know the offer is there. Remember to introduce yourself.
17. The visually-impaired person won't know if there is a spot on his tie or her slip is showing. If something needs attention, quietly let the person know about it.
18. Most visually-impaired people require assistance with banking, business correspondence and personal letters, but try not to take over. Letters and documents should always be handed to the person. He will ask for assistance if he needs it.
19. When you are introduced to a visually-impaired person, be ready to shake hands. Your handshake conveys a message about you and your personality.
20. A visually-impaired person cannot see you nod or shake your head, so express yourself in words. Your smile can be heard in your voice.
21. Use face-to-face contact; many visually-impaired persons can discern your facial expressions.
22. The visually-impaired person may touch you on the arm to make certain he/she is gaining your attention. We use eye-contact to establish some sort of rapport in our conversations – they use touch contact.
23. Be aware of how you use your voice. Feelings of anger, happiness, resentment or acceptance can be detected by a visually-impaired person.
24. Write notes in bold letters using black felt pen.

Tips For Guiding a Person with Restricted Vision[8]

1. Guides should put out their hand or arm to make contact with the partially sighted or blind person.
2. Let the partially sighted or blind person take your arm. Don't push them ahead of you. They will feel the motion of your body and follow easily. This puts the blind person approximately one half step behind the guide, allowing more reaction time. A good thing to keep in mind is the partially sighted or blind person's shoulder should be directly behind the guide's shoulder. This minimizes body width.
3. When approaching a chair, sofa or bench the blind person should be led directly to it, his knees brushing the front of the seat, and allowed to seat himself.
4. When being led to a chair that is not facing him, the blind person should be allowed to contact the back of the chair with his free hand, then allowed to seat himself.
5. For seating in an auditorium, theater, or church, the guide pauses at the appropriate row, the blind person aligns himself alongside the guide, and then the guide initiates lateral movement into the row. The blind person may want to trail the back of his hand along the row of seats in front of him for more balance and security.
6. For stairways or curbs, the guide approaches them in a straight-on fashion. A pause in step or a slight squeeze of the elbow are ways to inform the blind person of steps or a curb. The guide should say whether the stairs are up or down to prevent trips or stumbles. The guide should also pause at the last step to indicate the end of the stairs. If the stairs are narrow or congested, the blind person could fall in behind the guide and put his hand on the guide's shoulder.
7. The guide should go first when getting on or off buses, planes or subways. The guide paves the way; the blind person can then sense where steps are and whether they are up or down.
8. When entering an elevator where space is limited, the

guide and the blind person step into the elevator, release grip, then both guide and blind person turn inward and around to face the elevator door. The blind person then grips the arm of the guide in preparation for exit. This procedure is used in any situation where direction of travel has to be reversed, such as in hallways or public gatherings.

9. When passing through narrow passageways, such as doors or aisles, the guide moves his arm back as far as possible to give a definite signal for the blind person to move or fall in directly behind the guide in single file. Both guide and blind person are less likely to trip each other if the blind person extends the arm holding the guide.
10. When approaching doors, after signalling the blind person to fall in behind, the guide should state whether the door opens to the right or the left, and whether it swings in or out. This enables the blind person to make adjustments so that they can assist in holding the door open.
11. When assisting a blind person to enter a car, guide them to the door of the car and place their hand on the door handle. The blind person can then open the door which, by its swing, will tell them which direction the car is facing. Before entering, the blind person may want to put their other hand on the top of the car to judge the height.
12. Describe the scenery. If you are walking with a blind person, tell him about his surroundings, the buildings along the street, an interesting store or some unexpected happening. If it interests you, it may interest him.

DEAF-BLINDNESS[9]

What it Means to be Deaf-Blind: A deaf-blind person's main handicap is neither his deafness nor his blindness, but the combination of both. Without auditory or visual feedback, it is easy for him to become frustrated and feel isolated because of the limited information he receives. The difficulties this dual loss imposes vary with each individual. The person's age at the onset of each loss, the degree of hearing or visual impairment and whether or not speech has been developed, are all factors.

Loss of sight and hearing alone need not affect a person's mental ability. A deaf-blind person is often fully capable of making his own decisions when he knows what is going on around him and what his choices are. He wants to exercise his own initiative and live as normally as possible.

To accomplish this, another person is necessary. This other person becomes an extension of the deaf-blind individual, providing the opportunity to learn, succeed in work, participate in recreational and cultural activities and socialize. He or she is the means by which a deaf-blind person remains in the mainstream of society.

A warm firm hand clasp is as good as a smile. A show of interest is a physical pressure that says "I'm listening." Your hands are his eyes and ears; make them as observant and informative as possible.

Upon Meeting a Deaf-Blind Person:

1. Let him know by a gentle touch that you are present.
2. If he is a stranger, PRINT your message with your fingertip in block letters on the palm of his hand so he 'feels' the letters you are making. If he is someone you may meet again, try to learn his method of communication, no matter how slow you may be at first.
3. Let him know if you are alone or in the presence of other people. Identify yourself and establish a sign so he will recognize you readily when you meet again.
4. Be sure that the deaf-blind person understands what you are saying, and that you understand him in return, even if repeating several times is necessary.
5. Encourage him to use his voice if he has speech, even if he knows only a few words.
6. Address a deaf-blind person directly, not through someone else, reflecting the same courtesy you would a seeing, hearing person.
7. When walking, let him take your arm, never push him

ahead of you. Let him know when you are leaving him, even if for a brief moment.

8. Manual communication is easier to give than to receive. Take your time and be patient.

THE SPEECH IMPAIRED

If you haven't read the first section of this Chapter entitled, "Attitude Makes the World Different," please do so before reading on.

What is a Stroke?[10] A stroke occurs when the blood supply to a part of the brain tissue is cut off and, as a result, the nerve cells in that part of the brain cannot function. The nerve cells of the brain control the way we receive and interpret sensations and most of our bodily movements. When some of the nerve cells in the brain are not able to function, then the part of the body controlled by these nerve cells cannot function either.

The result of a stroke may be, for example, a difficulty in speaking, an inability to walk, or a loss of memory. The effects of a stroke may be very slight or they may be severe. They may be temporary or they may be permanent. It depends in part on which brain cells have been damaged, how widespread the damage is, how effectively the body can repair its system of supplying blood to the brain and how rapidly other areas of brain tissue can take over the work of the damaged brain cells.

What a person is like before he has a stroke will determine to some degree how he will react afterward, although stroke can mask or magnify personality traits. One patient will struggle to overcome his handicap, while another resigns himself to helplessness and requires much encouragement from others, especially the family. Recovery from stroke is dependent upon the brain damage, the general health of the patient, his personality and emotional state, support of those dear to him, and, of course, the care he receives.

Importance of Family The patient's family is his most important source of long-term support during the rehabilitative process. The patient must have the will to recover and the desire to be independent. Families should know to what extent the patient has been affected, and what they will have to face as a result of his illness. This period of adjustment may be difficult for both patient and family, but understanding his condition and being prepared for it does help. Then realistic goals can be set for the patient.

An increasing number of heart associations are conducting stroke programs to help families and communities cope with the problems of strokes. They are of great value to family members.

Understanding Aphasia Imagine waking up some morning and as you begin to speak the world seems to have turned topsy-turvy. People can't understand what you are saying. You attempt to say one word and a different one comes out. Perhaps you can't talk at all, no matter how hard you try. When someone speaks to you, it may sound like nonsense. The man or woman with the condition called aphasia may begin by having an experience just like this one. Suddenly he lives in a world of "scrambled" communication.

Aphasia (a-fa-zhia) is the technical name given for interference with the comprehension and use of language – a condition which can follow injury to the brain. Most cases of aphasia occur after a stroke, although many people with strokes do not become aphasic. Or aphasia can develop from other conditions where brain damage is present.

The first step in understanding the asphasic person is to recognize that he must be treated as someone with not a single problem but with a whole series of them. Your awareness of the extent of his difficulties will aid you in helping him. Aphasic patients who later recover say that one of their most distressing experiences was the failure of those around them to realize what a tremendous handicap they had.

Effective Communication With the Aphasic Individual[11]

Keep in mind that the following suggestions are general guidelines and may not apply to all aphasic individuals.

1. *Provide a positive environment that will encourage the aphasic individual to speak again.* Accept and praise all attempts to communicate, and encourage the individual to combine verbal statements, whenever possible, with

gestures such as pointing, nodding and shaking his head yes and no.

2. *Avoid verbal and nonverbal behavior that makes the person feel guilty for not speaking.* It is particularly important to avoid demonstrating impatience, irritability, or anger when the aphasic individual does not speak or understand as well as you think he should. Try to vent these feelings somewhere else when they occur.

3. *Try to accept the individual at his level of functioning and build on that.* This implies limiting goals to those that are realistic and can be reached in a short time. Unrealistic goals can only create a sense of failure. Reaching one realistic goal will motivate the aphasic individual to strive for the next.

4. *Point out the progress the patient is making.* Draw simple comparisons between current progress and the level of speech at the onset of aphasia. This will encourage the individual to feel more positive about making the effort to speak. Don't offer false hope to the patient (or yourself) but don't be pessimistic either. Remember that the goal is the maximum recovery possible. Working toward that goal with a mixture of patience and reality is the correct formula.

5. *Arrange for the patient to be seen and evaluated by a speech pathologist (preferably about two weeks after the trauma has occurred).* The results of this evaluation will indicate a realistic prognosis and will help determine an appropriate therapy program. Don't force the individual to participate in speech therapy, but do everything possible to help him want to work, through therapy, to improve his communication skills. Showing pleasure and praise for his efforts encourages the desire to improve.

6. *Try not to answer for the aphasic individual.* Give him the opportunity to speak and the time to come up with the right words when asked a question. Avoid interrupting him when he tries to say something. If the words spoken are understandable, don't correct the pronunciation or grammar. The aphasic individual's self-confidence may already be fragile.

7. *If the individual cannot find the word he wants and becomes frustrated, try to show empathy and understanding.* Tell him you know it must be frustrating and allow him an opportunity to express his feelings. Don't ever tell a patient, "You shouldn't feel that way."

8. *Don't pretend to understand the individual when you don't really comprehend what he's trying to say.* Pretending usually does not fool anyone, including the aphasic patient. He is working hard to communicate and deserves your best effort to understand. Ask him to "say it another way," repeat, or use gestures. Try playing "twenty questions" and attempt patiently to guess what he's trying to express.

9. *Get the aphasic individual's attention before beginning to speak.* Attempt to reduce noise, excessive movement, or other distractions when communicating with him.

10. *Speak according to the individual's ability to understand and respond.* If the patient is an adult, address him as an adult – not as a child.

11. *Try to avoid long sentences, rapid speech, or difficult and uncommon words.* Instead, communicate one idea at a time in clear, short sentences using everyday words. Allow as much as ten to fifteen seconds for these words to be processed.

12. *Don't speak in a loud voice unless the individual has experienced a hearing loss.* If there is a hearing loss, try to stand on the person's "good side" when speaking, and do not shout. Encourage him to use a hearing aid if one is needed or available.

13. *Use gestures and face the aphasic individual when you speak.* For example, as you say, "Do you want coffee?" point to the coffee pot or act out sipping from a cup.

14. *Don't ask the individual or anyone in his presence too many questions at one time or repeat the same question too quickly.* Also, don't have more than one person speak at a time. Remember that the aphasic individual wants to be included and needs time and concentration to process information or to formulate a response.

15. *If the individual can write better than he can speak, encourage him to use this means of communication. Similarly, if he can read better than he can understand spoken language, communicate with him in writing.*

16. *Don't discuss the aphasic individual in his presence as if he were a bedpan or a sick horse.* Quite often, the individual can understand some of what is being said even if he cannot respond. It is important to remember that his feelings are still intact, and he can be embarrassed, humiliated, hurt, or frustrated just as you can.

17. *Give the individual many opportunities to hear speech.* This helps him practice listening and may encourage him to attempt speech. Listening to radio or television may be useful in moderation. Be sensitive, however, to the possibility that radio, TV, and social interaction may be tiring to the aphasic individual in extended doses.

18. *Work out a set of signals with the individual for nonverbal cues that can prove helpful in daily conversations.* For instance, you can develop signals that indicate the individual wants or does not want you to say a word for him, or a signal such as the patient touching his ear to indicate that he wants you to speak louder. Such signals can be very practical in that they send a clear, quick message without interrupting the ongoing flow of conversation.

19. *If there is a communication board available, use it.*

20. *Encourage the patient to participate in normal and community social activities to the best of his abilities.* Be sensitive, however, to the fact that while the social interaction is very helpful, the aphasic individual may tire more quickly than formerly. If the aphasic individual is disoriented or confused, limit social contacts with visitors to those the patient can recognize and feel comfortable with.

21. *Allow the aphasic individual to occupy himself in activities he enjoys even if the activity seems futile or meaningless to you.* Permit him to be as independent as he wishes. This sense of freedom can be a very positive morale factor. However, it is helpful to set up and maintain a rou-

tine daily schedule that is familiar and nonstressful to the individual. Try to eliminate as many unknowns as possible. Stop and think, "What do I know that the patient needs or would like to know?" This applies to things like the day's schedule, the menu for dinner, what's happening in the news, or when guests are coming, as well as to larger, more frightening issues.

22. *Always explain to the aphasic individual what has happened to him and what will be happening next.* Repeat this information as often as necessary.

23. *Attempt to include the individual's input into major decisions affecting his life, but don't bother him with unnecessary problems and details.*

24. *Recognize that everyone is an important member of the treatment team, including the patient.* Family, friends, physicians, therapists and all other involved professionals have the same goal – maximum recovery. It is the task of the friend and family member to follow the advice and suggestions of the professionals; to ensure that they get the answers and information they need in order to do this well; to encourage the patient to begin and to continue prescribed speech and other therapies; and to provide appropriate support, encouragement and social interaction with the aphasic individual. It is the responsibility of the physician and other professionals to discipline themselves to a team approach and to see that the non-professional members of the individual's support system are treated as valuable co-equals on the team.

25. *Educate family and friends as to the nature of the aphasic individual's problems and to the ways in which they can be helpful.* For example, help them understand that they must give the individual time both to process what they have just said and to form an appropriate response.

26. *Beware of a tendency among family and friends to prescribe therapy for the aphasic individual.* Sometimes well-meaning attempts to be helpful can simply frustrate the patient. Follow the professional's recommendations for activities and appropriate rehabilitation materials. Keep home therapy sessions short and make them as successful as possible.

27. *Avoid letting your own needs and feelings become confused with those of the aphasic individual.* For example, a wish to protect the individual from situations that "might embarrass him" may actually reflect your own avoidance of situations where his behavior or condition may be embarrassing to you. Watch for this tendency and deal with it honestly if and when it occurs.

28. *Don't expect the aphasic individual to appreciate all of your efforts and good intentions.* If you are hurt by his lack of appreciation, it may be appropriate to examine your motives to make sure your efforts do not carry a hidden price tag. Also, don't try to make the individual meet all of your expectations and don't try to meet all of his. Except in rare situations, the aphasic person will never again perform in every way as he did before the brain damage occurred. Letting go of the past and building on the basis of the present can be a very positive experience of growth and maturity.

29. *Finally, and perhaps most important, it is essential to avoid letting other people's lives revolve around meeting the needs of the aphasic individual. For family members particularly, the best counsel is to take care of your own physical and emotional health. Taking care of yourself means that, in the long run, you will be in the best position possible to help the patient.* Arrange things so that you can have time to yourself. Stay in touch with your feelings. When you feel isolated and confined, don't play the martyr. When you feel frustration, anger, and resentment toward the aphasic individual, simply acknowledge these feelings as normal and don't allow yourself to feel guilty or "bad." Talk to a friend, minister, or professional counselor and "blow off steam." That is all part of emotional health.

Be aggressive in locating and enlisting the help of others. Join a stroke club or some other form of support group for patients, family, friends, clergy and professionals. If there is no such group in your area, start one. These groups enhance everyone's understanding of the problems of living with aphasia and form a vital support system.

A GUIDE TO WHEELCHAIR ETIQUETTE[12]

Meeting someone in a wheelchair should not be an awkward situation. However, many people are unsure of how to act, which can create some embarrassing moments. The following hints will help prepare you for encounters with wheelchair users. The tips also apply to those who care for patients in wheelchairs.

1. Ask permission. Always ask the wheelchair user if he or she would like assistance before you help. It may be necessary for the person to give you some instructions. An unexpected push could throw the wheelchair user off balance.

2. Be respectful. A person's wheelchair is part of his or her body space and should be treated with respect. Don't hang or lean on it unless you have the person's permission.

3. Speak directly. Be careful not to exclude the wheelchair user from conversations. Speak directly to the person. If the conversation lasts more than a few minutes, sit down or kneel to get yourself on the same plane as the wheelchair. Also, don't be tempted to pat a person in a wheelchair on the head as it is a degrading gesture.

4. Give clear directions. When giving directions to a person in a wheelchair, be sure to include distance, weather conditions and physical obstacles which may hinder a wheelchair user's travel.

5. Act natural. It is okay to use expressions such as "running along" when speaking to a person in a wheelchair. It is likely the wheelchair user expresses things the same way.

6. Wheelchair use doesn't mean confinement. Be aware that persons who use wheelchairs are not confined to them. When a person transfers out of the wheelchair to a chair, toilet, car or other object, do not move the wheelchair out of reaching distance.

7. Children are okay. Don't discourage children from asking questions about wheelchairs and disabilities. Children have a natural curiosity that needs to be satisfied so they do not develop fearful or misleading attitudes. Most wheelchair users are not offended by questions children ask them about their disabilities or wheelchairs.
8. Some wheelchair users can walk. Be aware of a wheelchair user's capabilities. Some users can walk with aids, such as braces, walkers or crutches, and use wheelchairs to conserve energy and move about more quickly.
9. Wheelchair users aren't sick. Don't classify persons who use wheelchairs as sick. Although wheelchairs are often associated with hospitals, they are used for a variety of non-contagious disabilities.
10. Relationships are important. Remember that persons in wheelchairs can enjoy fulfilling relationships which may develop. They have physical needs like everyone else.
11. Wheelchair use provides freedom. Don't assume that using a wheelchair is in itself a tragedy. It is a means of freedom which allows the user to move about independently.

Additional Tips on Wheelchair Etiquette

- Don't approach the person from behind and begin to push the wheelchair without first telling the person who you are. It can be frightening to be sitting still and suddenly be moving.
- Before moving a person make sure the footrests are locked and open.
- Check that the person's feet are securely on the footrests; that arms, hands and fingers are not near the wheel spokes; and that the brakes are released.
- When you stop – put the brakes on.
- Report any need of wheelchair repair to the person in charge.
- Going up a curb:
  1. Stop when you reach the curb.

2. Step firmly on the tipping lever and at the same time pull back and down on the handlebars.
3. Then move the wheelchair forward until the small wheels pass over the curb and the large rear wheels come in contact with the curb.
4. By leaning forward and pulling up on the handlebars, you can lift the wheelchair over the curb.
5. Going down, back the wheelchair over the curb.

THE MENTALLY IMPAIRED

The word "senile" is often used to describe older people who have misplaced their glasses, act confused or don't answer questions as quickly as they used to. Senile actually means "old," it does not mean forgetful, confused or crazy. Some memory loss or forgetfulness is a normal part of aging. As people move toward their eighties they may begin to lose their more recent memory and therefore start to live in and talk more about the past. They may forget what they have just had for lunch an hour ago, but be able to describe in vivid detail experiences of seventy-five years ago.

If there is little else in their lives to stimulate them, their thoughts seem to center on themselves, and physical infirmities take on greater importance. The old person may therefore forget to ask about the well-being and lives of others.

Normal forgetfulness is usually not enough to interfere drastically with their lives. Memory aids can be of great help for some, for example, written schedules, signs, appointment calendars, daily diaries or timers.

What many people mean when they use the word senile is really dementia. Dementia means a loss of mental abilities and is not a normal part of aging. There are reversible and irreversible dementias. For example, thyroid disease may cause a dementia that can be reversed by correcting the thyroid condition. Alcohol-induced dementia characterized by confusion can be treated in many cases.

Alzheimer's disease seems to be the most common cause of irreversible dementia. The next most common is multi-infarct dementia, Transient Ischemic Attacks (TIA's), a series of small strokes, sometimes so tiny that the person is unaware of them. It is important not to assume that people have Alzheimer's disease without first having a medical assessment.

Alzheimer's Disease[13]

Alzheimer's (pronounced altz'himerz) disease is a little-known but remarkably common disorder that affects the brain cells. It produces intellectual impairment in adults. While experts formerly believed that the disease occurred mainly in persons under age 65, this disorder is now recognized as the most common cause of severe intellectual impairment in older people as well. The changes most commonly associated with Alzheimer's disease occur in the proteins of the nerve cells in the cerebral cortex – the outer layer of the brain – leading to an accumulation of abnormal fibers. It is an inexorable, degenerative neurological disorder for which there is currently no known method of prevention or cure.

The fact that many people have never heard of Alzheimer's disease does not mean that it is a rare illness. Many individuals who have the disease never receive a precise diagnosis. The best current estimates indicate that more than three million North Americans may suffer from it.

At first, the individual with Alzheimer's disease experiences only minor and almost imperceptible symptoms that are often attributed to emotional upsets or other physical illnesses. Gradually, however, the person becomes more forgetful, particularly about recent events. The individual may neglect to turn off the oven, may misplace things, may continually recheck to see if a task was done, may take longer to complete a chore that was previously routine, or may repeat already answered questions. As the disease progresses, memory loss worsens and other manifestations such as confusion, irritability, restlessness and agitation are likely to appear, as well as changes in personality, mood and behavior. Judgement, concentration, orientation and speech may also be affected. Eventually, the disease renders its victims totally incapable of caring for themselves.

Although the person with Alzheimer's disease may deny or be unaware of the full extent of his or her limitations – especially later in the course of the illness – the seemingly unexplainable changes in essential functions are a source of deep frustration, both for the afflicted and for the caregivers.

Before a diagnosis of Alzheimer's disease is made, other illnesses which may cause the same symptoms must be excluded. The condition must be differentiated from the mild and occasional forgetfulness that sometimes occurs during normal aging. Depression, which is fairly common in elderly individuals facing a variety of stressful situations, may also present symptoms.

Each person suspected of having the disease should have thorough physical, neurological and psychiatric or psychogeriatric evaluations. After other diseases have been ruled out, in particular the dementia associated with previous strokes (multi- infarct dementia), a diagnosis can usually be made on the basis of medical history, mental status and the course of the illness. Periodic neurological examinations and psychological testing are very useful in confirming the diagnosis and evaluating the stage of the disease.

Communicating with the Mentally Impaired: As already noted, the capacity to use and understand language deteriorates slowly and seriously, making other forms of communication gradually more important. Non-verbal means, such as facial expression, body position or tone of voice, should help to convey ideas. Similarly, as speech may change to a stream of words interspersed with only a few appropriate ones, the person will convey something through stance, tone or facial expression. Yet feelings still remain and the person may express his or her need for reassurance or complaints of pain without words. Remember always to look for the meaning behind behavior that is puzzling.

- When talking to the person, listen and observe the reaction carefully; from his or her words and actions you can sense the possible degree of understanding. In this way you can continue to communicate at the appropriate level of understanding and not make false assumptions. This prevents "talking down" and helps maintain dignity and respect for the individual.

- Use short, simple sentences, spoken slowly and clearly. Present one statement or question at a time, allowing plenty of time for response. If necessary, repeat your question exactly as you did before. Sometimes questions requiring an answer may confuse the person. Even the answer "yes" or "no" may be difficult, or may not really convey his or her wishes.

- An affirmative statement such as "Here is your fruit" may be preferable to "Would you like some fruit?" Where possible, "either-or" questions should be avoided. Suggestions should be made very clearly.
- Whenever possible, the speaker should be in front of the person to maintain eye contact. Calling him or her by name should direct attention to your verbal exchange. Whenever practical, reinforce the spoken message using real objects and demonstration.
- You should also share with other caregivers any and all effective ways of communicating. This will make things easier for all concerned.

8
Things To Do Together

One can stand almost anything except a succession of ordinary days. – Goethe

Participating in the life of an elderly institutionalized person involves immeasurable commitment and emotional and physical stress that often continues for years until the elderly person dies. At the same time, it can be satisfying and enjoyable. No doubt it is a difficult task to dream up – day after day, week after week, year after year – things to do together that will be stimulating and add some zest to life. Don't forget about yourself. The activities you choose need to be, at least in part, something that you're interested in and enjoy.

I often tell people that my father never did anything for me. That usually gets me a curious look, and then I continue, but he did everything with me. And that is the message of this chapter. Knowing the interests of your elderly relative helps, and if you don't know, it makes wonderful conversation to find out. Take to the activities an attitude of doing with, not for, and don't be surprised if you find yourself less burdened and weary after your visit. You may also sense that both you and your relative are enjoying your visits more, possibly for the first time.

SELECTING MEANINGFUL ACTIVITIES

A Word of Caution: Elderly people are unique individuals, with their own interests and desires. Therefore it is important to think about what your relative or friend may want to do and discuss it with them. Some would just like to talk about what they've been doing or about themselves. Some would prefer to listen to your news. Some want to go on an outing and others have decided to withdraw from the mainstream of people and activity.

Participating in activities and special event days is important to some elderly residents, but not all. Cajoling and badgering an old person into participating in an activity may work. They may give in to your pressure when you tell them how good it would make them feel. But they don't necessarily agree because it's good for them: it may be that it's easier to agree than to assert themselves and tell you "no." In this situation no one is the better.

Need for Activities: For some elderly a better quality of life is maintained if they are able to continue their life-long hobby or interest. Older people who are losing their hearing or vision or are developing arthritic hands are not able to do things the way they have been accustomed to. Allow them to proceed at their own pace. If they are reluctant to participate, there may well be a good reason. They may be afraid of being embarrassed if they are not able to cope. They need to be encouraged and reassured that the extra effort is worthwhile. The attitude that we, as visitors, take is critical. If we participate with our elderly relatives, taking along a special dose of love and understanding, we will be making life more enjoyable for the older person.

Suggestions for Interests and Hobbies

- outdoor activities
- bird watching
- photography
- games and puzzles
- education
- painting and drawing, clay modelling
- entertainment
- reading
- creative writing
- drama
- music
- handicrafts (weaving, quilting, crocheting, stuffed toys, model-making, decoupage, macrame)
- coin or stamp collecting
- braided rugs
- wood working, wood carving, wood burning
- gardening indoors and outdoors
- puttering
- scrap books
- needlework

SHARING

Here are some activities you may try. Share them with your elderly relative as you would with any other friend or family member. Many of the suggestions listed here will provide much needed sensory stimulation:

Bring photographs and scrapbooks, old home movies, slides and look at and talk about them together;

Decorate your relative's room together the way they would like it decorated. Talk with the staff about hanging pictures, putting up a nice calendar, sewing some new curtains. Possessions are important and although there is not a lot of space it's amazing what you can do to help make it "their place;"

Help your relative at meal times if they have difficulty feeding themselves, but only if it's comfortable for both of you;

Help develop creative interests – assist them in poetry, calligraphy, drawing;

Help continue a life-long hobby or start a new one. Build a model airplane together, look at the stamp collection;

Share a project: knitting for the church bazaar or the new grandchildren; sorting out all the family slides and photographs;

Watch a show together;

Eat a meal together in the cafeteria;

Bake a cake or cookies together;

Play games;

Read out loud;

Listen to music together, preferably something both parties can enjoy;

Sew, mend or darn socks together;

Bring some of your work from home and have your elderly relative help you;

Share the Happy Hour or pub night together. If your facility doesn't have one, help start one;

Exercise together; ask the therapist to suggest some exercises. Activities that involve some physical activity are very important for older persons. If possible go for a walk, go swimming together. You may get some exercise for yourself;

Attend scheduled activities together; check the activities schedule that is posted and talk to the activity director;

Fill out necessary forms together – they can be very complicated and confusing;

Help write an autobiography. If the elderly person needs help with writing, you could write them down, or make a tape recording;

Start a newsletter for residents and visitors, together;

Build a suggestion box for residents and visitors, together;

Make a family collage together;

Clean out your recipe boxes together.

HELPING WITH DAILY TASKS

There is never enough staff, time or money to ensure that every resident is being looked after in the way we wish they could be or should be. Some staff members realize this and appreciate the interest that family members take. Sharing in daily tasks with the elderly can increase the satisfaction of visiting for both visitor and residents. Personal grooming is important. There are many things you can do with your relative to help them look better and feel better. You and I usually feel better when we're looking good; for many of us that takes a great amount of time and effort. Some tasks are listed here but you know others suited to your relative's needs and desires:

- hair care, set or permanent;
- manicure;
- shave;
- mend, wash, iron clothes;
- tidying room and closet;
- filling out menus;
- sorting out makeup;
- labeling clothes;
- helping them pay bills.

GIFTS AND GIVING

> *We should give of ourselves with the radiant warmth of sunshine and the glow of the open fire. The finest gift a man can give to his age and time is the gift of a constructive and creative life.* – author unknown

Everyone enjoys receiving gifts, even when the reply is "Oh, you shouldn't have done that" or "You shouldn't spend your money on me." They actually mean to say thank you, but sometimes gifts are difficult to receive no matter how small or how extravagant they are. Gifts are important and they need not be expensive. Some thoughts and suggestions about gift-giving follow:

Gifts show the elderly person that you care, that you have been thinking about them and that you've put in that little extra effort that makes them feel special. Preparing gifts only takes a few minutes and needn't cost a cent. Indeed, expensive gifts may make an elderly person feel indebted to you. As well, there is often no place to safely store expensive gifts. Always make sure personal possessions and clothes are marked.

Gifts can help maintain or develop new interests. Try to think of what the elderly person would really like or want or need when choosing a gift. Consider the elderly person's handicaps or disabilities (if any) when choosing a gift.

Gifts should not be a substitute for the gift of your company nor should they be given to compensate for guilt feelings. The only kind of giving which you can omit is giving advice.

Gift Suggestions

- warm bed jacket, lingerie, robe, slippers
- shawl, cardigan, bed socks, afghan
- shaving cream, unscented lotion
- brush, comb, easel-type mirror
- costume jewellery
- cards, cribbage set, checkers, jigsaw puzzles, chess, crosswords, joke book, find-a-word, book of Solitaire games
- magazines, large print books, folding book holder
- subscription to magazines, daily newspapers or book clubs
- writing paper, envelopes, stamps, return address labels

- pen, pencil, eraser, scrap-book and glue
- personalized stationery
- special needles, wool, sewing kit
- shoe polish, brush and shoe laces
- wrapping paper, string, tape, scissors
- photograph album, guest book
- clock with large numbers and illuminated face
- radio, tape recorder, cassettes
- seed catalogue, calendar
- phone coupons for long-distance, taxi gift certificates
- gift certificate for a new hairdo, manicure or pedicure
- season's tickets to the theatre
- binoculars and bird book
- calligraphy set, watercolours, drawing paper, charcoal

Food Gifts: First check about any special dietary restrictions with the staff.

- jam, jelly, marmalade
- home-made cooking
- special tea bags
- fruit, dates, seedless grapes
- ice cream
- mint wafers, chocolates, but not chewy toffee

Plants and Flowers: Some elderly residents take great pleasure in watching their gardens grow. Plants can bring a life force into the room and the heart of an older person. Small bouquets in sturdy vases or small flowering plants are appreciated more than large ones mainly because space is often limited. Home-grown flowers and pretty colored leaves are favorites. Flowers can be a nice reminder of your visit. Some plants (daffodils, amaryllis, jonquil, Jerusalem cherry, Lily of the Valley) are poisonous and should not be given to confused people.

Gifts To Give Away: Bring things that the resident can share. You may have given something to your relative that they do not need or that they know some other resident may enjoy. It's important that you give your elderly relative permission to give away your gifts. They won't give them all away but they will find enormous joy in giving – just as you do.

Challenging Gifts

- forgiveness
- respect
- tolerance
- genuine listening
- patience
- touching/closeness
- love

Other Imaginative Gifts

Writing labels for cassette tapes or records (in large print with black felt pen);

A happy thought or singing a song;

A calendar with dates marked on of relatives' and friends' anniversaries and other important occasions;

A collection of greeting cards for each occasion, including stamped and addressed envelopes. The elderly person need only add a line or two;

Most residents will value your time more than your money. What you might like to receive if you were in your relative's situation may be very different from what they would like. If none of these seems quite right, *ask* what the person would like.

OUTINGS

Many elderly people want and need to get out of their all-too-familiar surroundings. They appreciate and enjoy a variety of outings, and if physically and mentally able they like to do the same kinds of things they have done throughout their lives.

One reason that many visitors don't take their elderly relatives out is because they cannot manage wheelchairs and walkers. The staff is there to help you with this equipment and will assist your relative in and out of the car. If you go for a drive and can't assist your relative out of the car for lunch – go to a drive-in and eat in the car. It's a great change and well worth the effort. Transportation is often required to take your relative to the doctor, dentist, lawyer, to church or to visit a friend. Combining a medical appointment with going out for lunch makes a nice visiting time. Here are some outings for you to consider:

- a drive in the car;
- a walk in the garden;
- a stroll around the Nursing Home;
- a shopping jaunt to a mall including lunch; bring a friend along;
- dinner at your home;
- dinner at a favorite restaurant;
- a drive through the old neighborhood;
- going to church;
- a picnic in the park or zoo and a stop for an ice cream cone;
- a visit to friends of the elderly person;
- a meeting of a religious or service group your elderly relative once belonged to;
- sporting events;
- art galleries, museums;
- concerts, plays, movies;
- sight-seeing tours around the city. Bus companies are a gold mine of information on local sites;
- a trip out of the city to pick blueberries or blackberries;
- local farmers' market.

If you can't take your elderly relative out into the community, then bring as much of the community in to them as possible. Take a picnic lunch to the home and eat it in the solarium. Visit other areas of the care facility – the cafeteria, another floor, gift shop, library, chapel, patio or lounge.

Errands: Some outings, assuming your relative is mobile, can be built around things you have to do for yourself and your family. You may have a day or two a month that you set aside for your business errands, including paying bills, banking or going to the post office. You could combine these with a few errands for your elderly relative, such as getting hearing aid batteries, having their false teeth adjusted, choosing library books, taking in their radio or clock for repair, arranging for next month's doctor's appointment. AND take your relative along for the ride.

Remember, however, that doing things this way does take considerably longer. Too much rushing around is not pleasant for an older person. My mother and I could handle one appointment, the post office and lunch out before she was "pooped." Doing errands with an elderly person can be productive and enjoyable if you plan the day in a realistic way.

GROUP ACTIVITIES

Group activities are important for some elderly, while others do not wish to participate. We all know that socializing is important for well-being. It is vital that elderly individuals help to plan the activities in the Home if they are able to. Group leaders should encourage participation and decision-making as many elderly people haven't been involved in group activities for a long, long time; some of them never were. Depending also on the degree of physical or mental ability, some elderly will be ready to try new activities and some will participate in more limited ways. Elderly persons should not be coerced into taking part in activities. They need to be encouraged and finally to be allowed the freedom of choice. And that choice should be respected.

Some suggestions for group activities:

- craft group
- drama group, choir, music group
- barbecue or picnic
- slide presentations
- films, movies
- reminiscing group
- wheelchair dancing
- current events group
- bible study group

If you decide to lead or address a group, here are some important points to remember:

- get everyone's attention before you start speaking;
- speak a little slower and a little louder than usual;
- make sure everyone can see you;
- seat hard of hearing persons near you;
- don't talk down to the elderly.

MUSIC

> *When I hear music I fear no danger, I am invulnerable, I see no foe. I am related to the earliest times, and to the latest.* – Henry D. Thoreau

Music serves every part of us – the social, physical, intellectual and emotional. For most elderly people one crucial aspect of music is the joy it brings. There is nothing quite like music to brighten up the dreariest of days. There are a variety of ways to enjoy music:

- sing-alongs, musical games and dances, hymn sings;
- entertainment – choirs or solo performers, concerts;
- joining, starting or accompanying a choir;
- singing with a few friends;
- listening to music, tapes or records;
- music therapy.

You can share your talent by sitting down at the piano with your relative by your side and gathering a few residents around for a half hour of singing. (Check with the staff before you start, there may be another activity scheduled.) A guitar is portable enough for you to carry into some of the bed-ridden residents' rooms and sing them a few songs before dinner. It will add tremendous joy to their day and they'll have memories of you that will last for days.

READING

> *You open doors when you open books – doors that swing wide to unlimited horizons of knowledge, wisdom and inspiration that will enlarge the dimensions of your life. Through books you can know the majesty of great poetry, the wisdom of the philosophers, the findings of the scientists . . .*
>
> – Author unknown

Find out what your elderly relative's reading interests are. Reading aloud from short stories, magazines or newspapers can be enjoyed by many elderly. Visually impaired persons may especially appreciate this. Some facilities have large print books, so do libraries. "Talking books" (recorded readings) are available from libraries, video or record stores, or associations for the blind. Read the Bible together or the old classics. Some elderly may want to read stories to their grandchildren.

SPECIAL DAYS AND SPECIAL EVENTS

Every month has "special days." These are wonderful opportunities to share with your elderly relative. For example: Mother's Day, Father's Day, Remembrance Day, and St. Patrick's Day.

Ethnic customs and religious beliefs are important to celebrate with your relative. If the nursing home's staff have not planned a special activity, why don't you help to plan one?

The Nursing Home may also celebrate special events that you can share with the elderly, such as:

- New Resident Tea;
- Fashion Show;
- Kids and You;
- Fitness Week;
- Pet Day;
- Bake and Craft Sale.

Plan a birthday or anniversary party in the lounge or cafeteria for your relative or a resident who has no family. Or take them home if possible.

SPIRITUAL/RELIGIOUS ACTIVITIES

Spiritual/religious life for many elderly persons is a very personal and important matter. You could assist in taking them to activities of their faith in the community or attend some activities together in the facility, including:

- hymn sings;
- religious services (in person or taped);
- bible study groups;
- memorial services and funerals.

GAMES

Games are stimulating to people of any age and can increase mental functioning and alertness and boost morale of elderly residents. Remember, however, that many elderly people never played games and some simply don't like them. Some enjoy playing and could teach you a game or two. Below are some games that you may enjoy together:

- jigsaw puzzles;
- crossword puzzles, anagrams;
- seek-and-find word puzzles;
- puzzle books;
- card games–rummy, canasta, cribbage, bridge, etc.;
- Trivial Pursuit;
- Scrabble, checkers, dominoes;
- board games–Parcheesi (Ludo), Snakes and Ladders;
- chess;
- word games - make them up.

EDUCATION

"You *can* teach an old dog new tricks." We read and hear a lot these days about life-long learning. Studies show us that most older people can continue learning until the end of their days. Elderly persons living in institutions are no exception and many of them benefit from the intellectual stimulation.

Some suggestions:

- slide presentations;
- World Adventure Tours;
- educational movies;
- library services;
- adult education programs;
- current event groups;
- Great Books discussions.

CHILDREN

> *There are only two lasting bequests we can hope to give our children. One of these is roots, the other, wings.* – Hodding Carter

Young people of all ages can make life a little more enjoyable for the old. From babies to teenagers they all have a place in the life of the elderly. In fact, if some of the visiting were to be spread around the extended family, many old people would have no cause to be lonely – although they may complain of being more tired. Children, grandchildren and great-grandchildren make very stimulating company for elderly persons who often have no contact with the young. Children benefit from knowing their roots. They do not need to be protected or sheltered from institutionalized elderly members of their family. Nor do children need to be prevented from attending funerals, as old age and death are a natural part of life.

The old and the young can and will enjoy each other if given a chance; both groups are an integral part of the family. Children can go through old photo albums and together with the grandparent identify pictures and send copies of them to other family members. Older grandchildren could tape or write memoirs of the past; they could run errands and visit on their own, or write letters if they live in another city. Demonstrating a positive attitude toward older people who may be impaired will "rub off"on children and ultimately help to change society's negative attitude toward the elderly.

PETS

Animals are family members too. Family pets may have been a part of the elderly persons' life for many years until they had to move into a Nursing Home. Many Homes now have their own family pets, often a cat or a feathered friend or two. They make wonderful company and have an amazing ability to accept the elderly residents as individuals. They give an unconditional love – a type of caring that knows no bounds.

Pet therapy is a new, but rapidly growing form of treatment to reach withdrawn, lonely, or confused residents. Some homes have started programs for regular visits from animals, arranged through the local humane society. There, a volunteer coordinator screens the animals and their owners. In this case the animal has the main part of the interview: his ears are pulled and fur ruffled, as a confused person might do, to check the dog's reaction.

Gisele and her large dog, Frisky Froo, visit a nursing home regularly. During their "walk through," residents have the opportunity to *reach out* and make contact with their animal visitor, something they may not do with people. Residents save bits of their dinner for Frisky Froo. He has a regular following and feels okay about his weight gain but wonders why he is never invited to the volunteer events. If there are no animal visiting programs in your area, consider starting one.

Epilog

To end this book by paying tribute to my mother was not something I had planned to do. She was going to be acknowledged at the beginning of the text for her support and encouragement throughout the writing of this book. In fact, I was looking forward to walking up the stairs of a bookstore, with her on my arm, stopping at *the* shelf and watching her face as she looked with total disbelief at the finished product.

The motivation and inspiration for this book began long before any writing took place, at the time of my father's illness and institutionalization. It seems very fitting however, to pay tribute to my mother, Mrs. Elsie Thompson, at the end of this book – after all, she always did have the final word. For me, a profound closure has occurred – not just the last pages of a project but an end of an era of involvement and commitment to my parents. My mother died during the writing of the final stages of this book on July 29, 1986.

I knew before we ventured on our annual holiday that the time had come to do something with my mother about an alternative living situation for her. All of the questions on relocation were foremost in my mind, for that is exactly what I was writing about. She had managed to live alone in her apartment for almost five years after my father's institutionalization and death. Having been through the process and "system" with my father, I can only say now that I am thankful and relieved to be spared going through it all over again.

My mother and I were holidaying together at our summer home on the beautiful Lake of the Woods; I was writing the final parts of this book. My mother would have turned eighty in a few days. How wonderful that she spent her last days picking daisies and black-eyed susans (even some weeds) at the place she loved most. A row around the bay, the heron stalking the shore. She watched our duck family at their morning training session on the back dock, loons, hummingbirds at the feeder and her favorite, the chickadees. They all came to see her and to say goodbye.

A heart attack and a massive stroke. We spent her final two weeks together in the hospital. Although she couldn't talk or hear, she was at times aware and responsive, regaining consciousness just long enough for us to share some very precious, unspoken time together. I already have comforting memories – particularly the memory of the love that passed between us while she was dying. I cannot help telling you how very lucky I was to be there – holding her as she peacefully died. One day, I hope you too will have the opportunity of experiencing this profound life event.

My mother was a courageous, strong woman who started going deaf in her early twenties and eventually became almost totally deaf. She used to joke, saying, "You kids are lucky, all I got for an inheritance was these two deaf ears," but life, for the most part, was not a joking matter for my mother. As for many handicapped people, life had its unique struggles. Now she is free. I am comforted to believe that she is now hearing the music of angels – what a beautiful and joyful sound that must be.

Appendix

The following is a representative list of health information organizations, professional associations, consumer organizations and associations that deal with the special concerns of the elderly. There are hundreds of smaller organizations that may suit your specific needs. To find their address and telephone number check at a main library for the following directories:

Canada: *Directory of Associations in Canada* by Micromedia.

United States: *The Encyclopedia of Associations, 1987 edition* by editor Katherine Gruber (Gale Research Company);

Great Britain: *Directory of British Associations and Associations in Ireland, 9th Edition* by G. P. Henderson and S. P. A. Henderson (eds). Kent: CBD Research Ltd., 1987;

Republic of Ireland: *Administration Yearbook and Diary* by the Institute of Public Administration, Dublin.

HEALTH INFORMATION ORGANIZATIONS

There are literally hundreds of organizations and agencies that can provide further information and assistance to you. Many of the following organizations are not primarily for the elderly, but will be helpful to those with specific medical conditions. Some provide support groups while others also provide financial and legal assistancc. Many have national, regional and local branches.

You can easily find local and regional offices through your telephone directories or Better Business Bureaus. If you live outside of an urban centre you can call, free. In North America dial *area code* + 555-1212 to get the branch office in the city nearest you.

Whenever you are in a hurry to get information, call these organizations directly and ask for information to be mailed First Class. If you receive information by phone always have a list of questions written out and write any answers on the same sheet of paper including the name of the person providing the information.

Every effort has been made to ensure that the addresses and phone numbers are up-to-date. Telephoning directly will ensure that you find out quickly if the organization has changed its address or telephone number.

CANADIAN

Alzheimer Society of Canada
1320 Yonge St., Suite 302
Toronto ON M4T 1X2
(416) 925-3552

The **Arthritis** Society
250 Bloor St. E., Ste. 401
Toronto ON M4W 3P2
(416) 967-1414

Canadian National Institute
for the **Blind**
1929 Bayview Ave.
Toronto ON M4W 3P2
(416) 486-2500

Canadian **Cancer** Society
2 Carlton St., Ste. 710
Toronto ON M5B 2J2
(416) 593-1513

Canadian Coordinating Council
on **Deafness**
116 Lisgar St., Ste. 203
Ottawa ON K2P 0C2
(613) 232-2611

Canadian **Diabetes** Assoc.
78 Bond St.
Toronto ON M5B 2J8
(416) 362-4440

Canadian **Heart** Foundation
1 Nicholas St., Ste. 1200
Ottawa ON K1N 7B7
(613) 237-4361

Kidney Foundation of Canada
4060 St. Catharines St. W., Ste. 555
Montreal PQ H3Z 2Z3
(514) 934-4806

Canadian **Lung** Assoc.
75 Albert St., Ste. 908
Ottawa ON K1P 5E7
(613) 237-1208

Canadian **Mental Health** Assoc.
2160 Yonge St.
Toronto ON M4S 2A9

Parkinson Foundation of Canada
55 Bloor St. W., Ste. 232
Toronto ON M4W 1A6
(416) 484-7750

Canadian **Red Cross** Society
1800 Alta Vista Dr.
Ottawa ON K1G 3Y6
(613) 676-8000

Stroke (*See* Heart)

AMERICAN

Alzheimer's Disease and Related
Disorders Association
70 East Lake St., Ste. 600
Chicago, IL 60601
(312) 853-3060

The **Arthritis** Foundation
1314 Spring St. N.W.
Atlanta, GA 30309
(404) 872-7100

American Foundation for the **Blind**
15 West 16th St.
New York, NY 10011
(212) 620-2000

American **Cancer** Society
261 Madison Ave
New York, NY 10016
(212) 599-3600

National Association of the **Deaf**
814 Thayer Ave.
Silver Spring, MD 20910
(301) 587-1788

American **Diabetes** Association
1660 Duke St.
Alexandria, VA 22314
(703) 549-1500

American **Heart** Association
7320 Greenville Ave.
Dallas, TX 75231
(214) 750-5300

National **Kidney** Foundation
30 East 33rd St., 11th Floor
New York, NY 10016
(212) 889-2210

American **Lung** Association
1740 Broadway
New York, NY 10019
(212) 315-8807

National **Mental Health** Association
1021 Prince St.
Arlington, VA 22314
(703) 684-7722

American **Parkinson** Disease Association
116 John St., Ste. 417
New York, NY 10038
(212) 732-9550
or Toll Free (800) 223-APDA

American **Red Cross**
Washington, D.C. 20006
(202) 639-3220

Stroke (*See* Heart)

UNITED KINGDOM

Arthritis Care
6 Grosvenor Cres.,
London, SW1X 7ER
01-235 0902

Royal National Institute
for the **Blind**
224-228 Gt. Portland St.,
London, W1N 6AA
01-388 1266

Cancer Aftercare
& Rehabilitative Society
16 Stapleton Rd., Bristol, BS5 0QX
(0272) 553161

British **Deaf** Association
38 Victoria Pl., Carlisle, CA1 1HU
(0228) 20188

British **Diabetic** Association
10 Queen Anne St.,
London, W1M 0BD
01-323 1531

Chest, **Heart** & Stroke Association
Tavistock House N., Tavistock Sq.,
London, WC1H 9JE
01-387 3012

British **Kidney** Patient Association
Bordon, Haunts, GU35 9JS
(04203) 2021/2

Lung (*See* Heart)

MIND (National Association
for **Mental Health**)
22 Harley St., London, W1N 2ED
01-637 0741

Parkinson's Disease
Society of the United Kingdom Ltd.
36 Portland Pl., London, W1N 3DG
01-323 1174

British **Red Cross**
9 Grosvenor Cres.,
London, SW1X 7EJ
01-235 5454

Stroke (*See* Heart)

PROFESSIONAL ASSOCIATIONS

The following associations represent cross sections of professional associations and resource groups. Sometimes there is not a comparable organization in Canada, the United States, or Great Britian. You can check with your local telephone directories for local/regional branches.

American **Art Therapy** Association, Inc., 505 E. Hawley St., Mundelein, IL 60060, (312) 949-6064

British Association of **Art Therapists**, 13c Northwood Rd., London, N6 5TL

American Academy of **Family Physicians** 1740 W. 92nd St., Kansas City, MO 64114, (816) 333-9700

College of **Family Physicians** of Canada, 4000 Leslie St., Willowdale, ON M2K 2R9, (416) 493-7513

Royal College of **General Pracititioners**, 14 Prince's Gate, London, SW7 1PU, 01-581 3232

National Association for **Home Care**, 519 C St. N.E., Stranton Park, Washington, DC 20002, (202) 547-7424

American **Hospital** Association, 840 North Lake Shore Dr., Chicago, IL 60611, (312)280-6000

Association of General Practitioner **Hospitals**, Aldemoor Health Centre, Aldemoor Close, Southampton, S016ST, (0703) 783111

Canadian **Hospital** Association, 17 York St., Ste. 100, Ottawa, ON K1N 9J6, (613) 238-8005

American **Medical** Association, 535 North Dearborn St., Chicago, IL 60610, (312) 645-5000

British **Medical** Association, BMA House, Tavistock Sq., London, WC1H 9JP, 01-387 4499

Canadian **Medical** Association, 1867 Alta Vista Dr., Ottawa, ON K1G 3Y6, (613) 731-9331

British Society for **Music Therapy**, Guildhall School of Music & Drama, Barbican, London, EC24 8DT, 01-368 8879

National Association for **Music Therapy**, 505 11th St. S.E., Washington, DC 20003, (202) 543-6864

American **Nurses** Association, 2420 Pershing Road, Kansas City, MO 64108, (816) 474-5720

Canadian **Nurses** Association, 50 The Driveway, Ottawa, ON K2P 1E2, (613) 237-2133

UK Royal College of **Nursing**, 20 Cavendish Sq., London, W1M 0AB, 01-409 3333

American **Occupational Therapy** Association, Inc. 1383 Piccard Drive, Box 1725, Rockville, MD 20850, (301) 948-9626

British Association of **Occupational Therapists** Ltd., 20 Rede Pl., London, W2 4TU, 01-229 9738

Canadian Association of **Occupational Therapists**, 110 Eglinton Ave. W., 3rd Fl., Toronto, ON M4R 1A3, (416) 487-5404

American **Pharmaceutical** Association, 2215 Constitution Ave. N.W., Washington, DC 20037, (202) 628-4410

Canadian **Pharmaceutical** Association, 1785 Alta Vista Dr., Ottawa, ON K1G 3Y6, (613) 523-7877

Pharmaceutical Society of Great Britian, 1 Lambeth High St., London, SE1 7JN, 01-735 9141

American **Physical Therapy** Association, 1111 North Fairfax St., Alexandria, VA 22314, (703) 684-2782

Canadian **Physiotherapy** Association, 890 Yonge St., 9th Flr., Toronto ON M4W 3P4, (416) 924-5312

Chartered Society of **Physiotherapy**, 14 Bedford Row, London, MC1R 4ED, 01-242 1941

American **Psychiatric** Association, 1400 K. St. N.W., Washington, DC 20005, (202) 682-6000

Canadian **Psychiatric** Association, 294 Albert St., Suite 204, Ottawa ON K1P 6E6, (613) 234-2815

Royal College of **Psychiatrists**, 17 Belgrave Sq., London, SW1X 8PG, 01-235 2351

American **Psychological** Association, 1200 17th St. N.W., Washington, DC 20036, (202) 955-7600

British **Psychological** Society, 48 Princess Rd. E., Leicester, LE1 7DR, (0533) 549568

Canadian **Psychological** Association, Vincent Road, Old Chelsea, PQ J0X 2N0, (819) 827-3927

British Association of **Social Workers**, 16 Kent St., Birmingham, B5 6RD, 021-622 3911

Canadian Association of **Social Workers**, 55 Parkdale Ave., Ottawa, ON K1Y 1E5, (613) 728-1865

National Association of **Social Workers**, 7981 Eastern Ave., Silver Spring, MD 20910, (301) 565-0333

CONSUMER ORGANIZATIONS

Many consumer organizations are relatively young and staffed by volunteers. They provide useful information. You are recommended to check with many of them to determine which meets your specific needs before committing funds to any particular one.

Consumer Health Organization
280 Sheppard Ave., Ste. 207
Toronto ON M2N 3B1
(416) 674-7105

[Includes newsletter and information on alternative health therapies and referral to practitioners.]

Center for Medical Consumers
237 Thompson St.,
New York, NY 10012
(212) 674-7105

[Large, non-circulating library which critically evaluates health care professional information plus alternative medical treatments; publishes "Health Facts" newsletter.]

Consumers Association of Canada
Box 9300,
Ottawa, ON K1G 3T9
(613) 733-9450

[Published "Consumer's Rights in Health Care" statement.]

PATIENTS' RIGHTS AND EDUCATION:

There are numerous organizations dedicated to patients' rights. Check your local telephone directory, health care professional or library for one located in your region. Examples of such organizations are:

National Association for Patient Participation
Wyeval, School Rd., Godshill,
Ventor loW P038 3HJ
(0983) 840359

Patients Association
Rm. 33, 18 Charing Cross Rd.,
London, WC2H 0HR
01-240 0671

Patients' Rights Association (for Ontario)
40 Homewood Ave.,
Toronto, ON M4Y 2K2
(416) 923-9629

[Non-profit volunteer organization providing education and advise to Ontario patients. Also lobby government and regulatory bodies to extend and improve rights and complaint procedures.]

Peoples' Medical Society
14 E. Minor St.,
Emmaus, PA 18049
(215) 967-2136

[One of the fastest growing patient rights and education organizations in the United States with over 85,000 members. It is non-profit and provides information on patient rights, medical treatment and a newsletter. Publishers of Take This Book to the Hospital With You *by Charles B. Inlander and Ed Weiner.]*

ORGANIZATIONS CONCERNED WITH THE ELDERLY

Canadian Assoc. of Retired Persons
27 Queen St. East
Suite 304
Toronto ON (416) 363-8748

Canadian Institute of
Religion and Gerontology
40 St. Clair Ave. E., Suite 203
Toronto ON M4T 1M9
(416) 924-5865

Continuing Care Resources
P.O. Box 80688
South Burnaby BC V5H 3Y1

Gerontology Assoc. of Nova Scotia
50 Pleasant st.
P.O. Box 1312
Wolfville NS B0P 1X0
(902) 542-9327

Gerontology Research Council
of Ontario
88 Maplewood Avenue
Hamilton ON L8M 1W9
(416) 549-6525

National Advisory Council on Aging
Room 1264, Jeanne Mance Building
Tunney's Pasture
Ottawa ON K1A 0K9

Ontario Advisory Council on
Senior Citizens
700 Bay Street 2nd Floor,
Toronto ON M5G 1Z6
(416) 965-2324

Secretariat for Fitness
in the Third Age
c/o Canadian Parks and Recreation
Association
333 River Road
Ottawa ON K1L 8H9
(613) 748-5651

The Vanier Institute of the Family
120 Holland, Suite 300
Ottawa ON K1Y 0X6
(613) 722-4007

Recommended Readings

GENERAL INTEREST BOOKS

Although these books are recommended for the general public, they would also be useful for caregivers involved in the care and treatment of the elderly.

van Bommel, H., *Choices: For People Who Have a Terminal Illness, Their Families and Their Cargivers.* Toronto, ON: NC Press, 1987.

Booth, T., *Home Truths. Old People's Homes and the Outcome of Care.* Aldershot, England and Brookfield, Vermont, USA: Gower Publishing Company, 1985.

Brody, E. M. *Long-term Care of Older People. A Practical Guide.* New York and London: Human Sciences Press, 1977.

Brody, E. M., "'Women in the Middle' and Family Help to Older People." *The Gerontologist* 21(5):471-80, 1981.

Buckman, R., *I Don't Know What To Say: How To Help and Support Someone Who Is Dying.* Toronto, ON: Key Porter Books Ltd., 1988.

Carlin, Vivian, and Ruth Mansberg, *Where Can Mom Live? A Family Guide to Living Arrangements for Elderly Parents.* Lexington, MA: Lexington Books, 1987.

Cohen, S. Z., and B. M. Gans, *The Other Generation Gap – You and Your Aging Parents.* Chicago: Follett Publishing Co., 1978.

Comfort, A., *A Good Age.* New York: Simon and Schuster, 1976.

Feil, N., *Validation: The Feil Method, How to Help Disoriented Old-Old.* Cleveland: Edward Feil Productions, 1982.

Kansas State Department of Social and Rehabilitativc Services, *The Volunteer and the Older Person: A Handbook for Volunteers in the Field of Aging.* Topeka, Kansas: Services for the Aging, 1976.

Katz, Jay, M. D., *The Silent World of Doctor and Patient.* New York: The Free Press, 1984.

Mace, N. L. and P. V. Rabins, *The 36-Hour Day.* Baltimore: The Johns Hopkins University Press, 1981.

Sheehy, G., *Passages.* Toronto: Bantam Books, 1974.

Sheehy, G., *Pathfinders.* Toronto: Bantam Books, 1981.

Skinner, B. F. and M. E. Vaughan, *Enjoy Old Age.* New York: Warner Books, 1983.

Watt, J. and A. Calder, *Taking Care – A Self-Help Guide for Coping with an Elderly, Chronically Ill, or Disabled Relative.* Vancouver, BC: International Self-Counsel Press, 1986.

GENERAL INTEREST BOOKS FOR PROFESSIONAL CAREGIVERS

The resources listed below are more technical in nature and often written specifically for professional caregivers, but may also be interesting for non-professionals.

Aronson, J., "Family Care of the Elderly: Underlying Assumptions and Their Consequences." *Canadian Journal on Aging* 4(3):115-25, 1985.

Barton, M., *As We Are Now.* New York: W. W. Norton, 1973.

Bengsten, V., and E. DeTerre, "Aging and Family Relations." *Marriage and Family Review* 3:51-56, 1980.

Bennett, R., *Aging, Isolation and Re-Socialization.* New York: Van Nostrand Reinhold Company, 1980.

Berger, E. Y., "The Institutionalization of Patients with Alzheimer's Disease." *Danish Medical Bulletin* 32(1):71-76, 1985.

Berk, M. L., and G. R. Wilensky, "Health Care of the Poor Elderly: Supplementing Medicare." *The Gerontologist* 25(3): 311-14, 1985.

Borup, J. H., "Relocation: Attitudes, Information Network and Problems Encountered." *The Gerontologist* 21(5):501-11, 1981.

Brocklehurst, J.C., "Inculcation of Appropriate Attitudes and Skills." In A. N. Exton-Smith and J. Grimley Evans (eds.). *Care of the Elderly: Meeting the Challenge of Dependency.* London: Academic Press; New York: Grune and Stratton, 234-41, 1977.

Brody, E. M. "Environmental Factors in Dependency." In A. N. Exton-Smith and J. Grimley Evans (eds.). *Care of the Elderly: Meeting the Challenge of Dependency.* London: Academic Press; New York: Grune and Stratton, 81-95, 1977.

Brody, E. M., "The Etiquette of Filial Behaviour." *Aging and Human Development* 1:87-94, 1970.

Brody, E. M., H. Kleban, and M. Moss, "Measuring the Impact of Change." *The Gerontologist* 14:299-305, 1974.

Cantor, M. H., "Strain Among Caregivers: A Study of Experience in the United States." *The Gerontologist* 23(6):597-604, 1983.

Chappell, N. L., "Social Support and the Receipt of Home Care Services." *The Gerontologist* 25(1):47-54.

Chappell, N. L., and B. Havens, "Who Helps the Elderly Person: A Discussion of Formal and Informal Care." In W. A. Peterson and J. Quadagno (eds.). *Social Bonds in Later Life. Aging and Interdependence.* Beverly Hills, London, New Delhi: Sage Publications, 211-27, 1985.

Comfort, A., *Practice of Geriatric Psychiatry.* New York: Elsevier North Holland, Inc., 1980.

Crossman, L., C. London, and C. Barry, "Older Women Caring for Disabled Spouses: A Model for Supportive Services." *The Gerontologist* 21:464-70, 1981.

Denham, M. J. (ed.), *Care of the Long-Stay Elderly Patient.* London and Canberra: Croom Helm Ltd., 1983.

Dulude, L., *Women and Aging: A Report on the rest of our Lives.* Ottawa, ON: Canadian Advisory Council on the Status of Women, 1978.

Eisdorfer, C., "Mental Health Problems in the Aged." In A. N. Exton-Smith and J. Grimley Evans (eds.). *Care of the Elderly: Meeting the Challenge of Dependency.* London: Academic Press; New York: Grune and Stratton, 59-67, 1977.

Evans, J. G., "Current Issues in the United Kingdom." In A. N. Exton-Smith and J. Grimley Evans (eds.). *Care of the Elderly: Meeting the Challenge of Dependency.* London: Academic Press; New York: Grune and Stratton, 130-32, 1977.

Fengler, A. P., and N. Goodrich, "Wives of Elderly Disabled Men: The Hidden Patients." *The Gerontologist* 19:175-83, 1979.

Forbes, W. F., J. A. Jackson, and A. S. Kraus, *Institutionalization Of The Elderly In Canada.* Toronto, ON; Vancouver, BC: Butterworths, 1987.

Fox, M., and M. Lithwick, "Groupwork With Adult Children of Confused Institutionalized Parents." *Long-Term Care and Health Services Administration* 2:121-31, 1978.

Grant, P. R., "Who Experiences the Move into a Nursing Home as Stressful? Examination of the Relocation Stress Hypothesis Using Archival, Time-Series Data." *Canadian Journal on Aging* 4(2):87-100, 1985.

Greene, V. L., and D. J. Monahan, "The Impact of Visitation on Patient Well-Being in Nursing Homes." *The Gerontologist* 22(4):418-23, 1982.

Greenfield, W. L., "Distruption and Reintegration: Dealing with Familial Response to Nursing Home Placement." *Journal of Gerontological Social Work* 8(1/2):15-21, 1984.

Greer, D. S., V. Mor, J. N. Morris et al., "An Alternative in Terminal Care: Results of the National Hospice Study." *Journal of Chronic Diseases* 39(1):9-26, 1986.

Gutman, G. M. and N. K. Blackie (eds.), *Aging in Place: Housing Adaptions and Options for Remaining in the Community.* Burnaby, BC: The Gerontology Research Centre, Simon Fraser University, 1986.

Harel, Z., "Quality of Care, Congruence and Well-being Among Institutionalized Aged." *The Gerontologist* 21(5):523-31, 1981.

Havens, B., "Boundary Crossing: An Organizational Challenge for Community Based Long-Term Care Service Agencies." In A. O. Pelham, W. F. Clark (eds.). *Managing Home Care for the Elderly. Lessons from Community-Based Agencies.* New York: Springer Publishing Co., 77-98, 1986.

Helphand, M., and C. M. Porter, "The Family Group Within the Nursing Home. Maintaining Family Ties of Long-term Care Residents." *Journal of Gerontological Social Work* 4:51-62, 1981.

Johnson, C. L., and D. J. Catalano, "A Longitudinal Study of Family Supports to Impaired Elderly." *The Gerontologist* 23(6):612-18, 1983.

Johnson, E. S., and D. L. Spence, "Adult Children and Their Aging Parents: An Intervention Program." *Family Relations* January:115-22, 1982.

Kane, R. L., and R. A. Kane, "Long-term Care: Can Our Society Meet the Needs of Its Elderly?" *Annual Reviews Public Health* 1:227-53, 1980.

Kane, R. L., and R. A. Kane, *A Will and a Way. What the United States Can Learn From Canada about Caring for the Elderly.* New York: Columbia University Press, 1985.

Kartman, L. L., "People Helping People: Burnout." *Activities, Adaptation and Aging* 3(4):49-57, 1983.

Kasl, S. V., "Physical and Mental Health Effects of Involuntary Relocation and Institutionalization of the Elderly – a Review." *American Journal of Public Health* 62:377-84, 1972.

Kastenbaum, R., "The 4% Fallacy: A Methodological and Empirical Critique of Extended Care Facility Population Statistics." *International Journal of Aging and Human Development* 4(1), 1973.

Kayser-Jones, J. S., "Open-Ward Accommodation in a Long-Term Care Facility: The Elderly's Point of View." *The Gerontologist* 26(1):63-69, 1986.

Kraus, A. S., "The Burden of Care for Families of Elderly Persons with Dementia." *Canadian Journal on Aging* 3(1):45-51, 1984.

Kraus, A. S., R. A. Spasoff, E. J. Beattie, et al., "Elderly Applicants to Long-Term Care Institutions: I. Their Characteristics, Health Problems, and State of Mind." *Journals of the American Geriatrics Society* 24(3):117-25, 1976.

Kraus, A. S., R. A. Spasoff, E. J. Beattie, et al., "Elderly Applicants to Long-Term Care: II. The Application Process, Placement and Care Needs." *Journal of the American Geriatrics Society* 24(4):165-72, 1976.

Lemke, S., and R. H. Moos, "Qualiity of Residential Settings for Elderly Adults." *Journal of Gerontology* 41(2):268-76, 1986.

MacLean, M. J., and R. Bonar, "The Normalization Principle and the Institutionalized Elderly." *Canada's Mental Health* 31(2):16-18, 1983.

Mandelstam, D., *Incontinence and its Management.* London: Groom Helm Ltd., 1980.

Merrill, T., *Activities for the Aged and Infirm: A Handbook for the Untrained Worker.* Springfield, Illinois: Charles C. Thomas, 1967.

McGrother, C. W., C. M. Castleden, H. Duffin, and M. Clarke, "Provision of Services for Incontinent Elderly People at Home." *Journal of Epidemiology and Community Health* 40:134-38, 1986.

Mitchell, J. B., "Physician Visits to Nursing Homes." *The Gerontologist* 22(1):45-48, 1982.

Mitchell-Pedersen, L., L. Edmund, E. Fingerote, and C. Powell, "Let's Untie the Elderly." *OAHA Quarterly* (October):10-14, 1985.

Ontario Association of Homes for the Aged, *Guide to Caring for the Mentally Impaired Elderly.* Toronto: Methuen Publications, 1985.

Ordal, C. C., "To 'Grow Side By Side'." *Aging,* pp. 25-28, 1981.

Palmer E., and J. Watt, *Living and Working With Bereavement Guide for Widowed Men and Women.* Calgary, AB: Detselig Enterprises Ltd., 1987.

Palmore, E., "Total Chance of Institutionalization Among the Aged." *The Gerontologist* 16(6), 1976.

Posner, J., "Notes on the Negative Implications of Being Competent in a Home for the Aged." In J. Hendricks (ed.). *Institutionalization and Alternative Futures.* Perspectives on Aging and Human Development Series; 3. Farmingdale, New York: Baywood Publishing Company Inc., 138-45, 1980.

Preston, G. A. N., "Dementia in Elderly Adults: Prevalence and Institutionalization." *Journal of Gerontology* 41(2):261-67, 1986.

Reilley, G. M., "Visitation of Institutionalized Elderly by High School Students: Effects on Both Age Groups." *Psychology, Clinical* University of Nevada, Reno, 1976.

Reinke, B. J., D. S. Holmes, and N. W. Denney, "Influence of a 'Friendly Visitor' Program on the Cognitive Functioning and Morale of Elderly Persons." *American Journal of Community Psychology* 9(4):491-504, 1981.

Roozman-Weigensberg, C., and M. Fox, "A Groupwork Approach With Adult Children of Institutionalized Elderly: An Investment in the Future." *Journal of Gerontolotical Social Work* 2:355-62, 1980.

Rubin, A., and G. E. Shuttlesworth, "Engaging Families As Support Resources in Nursing Home Care: Ambiguity in the Subdivision of Tasks." *The Gerontologist* 23(6):632-36, 1983.

Safford, F., "A Program for the Families of the Mentally Impaired Elderly." *The Gerontologist* 20:656-60, 1980.

Shanas, E., "The Family As a Social Support System in Old Age." *The Gerontologist* 19:169-74, 1979.

Shuttlesworth, G. E., A. Rubin, and M. Duffy, "Families Versus Institutions: Incongruent Role Expectations in the Nursing Home." *The Gerontologist* 22(2):200-8, 1982.

Silverman, A. G., and C. Brahce, "'As Parents Grow Older': An Intervention Model." *Journal of Gerontological Social Work,* 2:77-85, 1979.

Snyder, L. H., P. Rupprecht, J. Pyrele, et al., "Wandering." *The Gerontologist* 18(3):272-80, 1978.

Steinman, L. A., *Predictors of Family Involvement Following Nursing Home Placement of an Older Parent.* Los Angeles: University of Southern California, 1982.

Struyk, R. J., and H. M. Katsura (eds.). *Aging at Home: How the Elderly Adjust Their Housing Without Money.* New York: The Haworth Press, 1988.

Wells, L., and G. Macdonald, "Interpersonal Networks and Post-Relocation Adjustment of the Institutionalized Elderly." *The Gerontologist* 21(2):177-83, 1981.

Wister, A. V., "Living Arrangement Choices Among the Elderly." *Canadian Journal on Aging* 4(3):127-44, 1985.

York, J. L., and R. J. Calsyn, "Family Involvement in Nursing Homes." *The Gerontologist* 17:500-5, 1977.

End Notes

The author would like to thank the following groups and associations for allowing the use of their informative publications.

Chapter One

1. Adapted from the article "Writings in Gerontology, No. 1, Family Role and the Negotiation of Change for the Aged," Government of Canada, National Advisory Council on Aging, Rm. 1264, Jeanne Mance Bldg., Ottawa, Canada, K1A 0K9.

2. From the brochure, *Freedom is Understanding Each Other,* The Canadian National Institute for the Blind, 1929 Bayview Ave., Toronto, ON, M4W 3P2, (416) 486-2500.

Chapter Three

1. Adapted from the brochure *Thinking About a Care Facility,* City of Vancouver Health Department, Long Term Care Program, Continuing Care Division, Ministry of Health, 1060 West 8th Ave., Vancouver, BC, V6H 1C4.

Chapter Six

1. Adapted from the brochure, *You and Your Doctor,* The British Columbia Medical Association and the doctors of the province, 115 - 1665 West Broadway, Vancouver, Canada, V6J 1X1.

Chapter Seven

1. From the brochure, *Hearing Loss in the Elderly,* The Canadian Hearing Society, 271 Spadina Rd., Toronto, Canada, M5R 2V3.

2. Adapted from the brochure, *Speechreading,* Vancouver League for the Hard of Hearing, 2125 West 7th Avenue, Vancouver, Canada, V6K 1X9.

3. Adapted from the article, "Common Misconceptions About Deafness," The Canadian Hearing Society.

4. (No. 1-9) adapted from the article "Communicating with a Hard of Hearing Person," The Canadian Hearing Society.

5. (No. 10-20) adapted from the article "Communicating with a Hard of Hearing Person," Vancouver League for the Hard of Hearing.
6. Adapted from the brochure, *Freedom is Understanding Each Other,* The Canadian National Institute for the Blind.

7. *Ibid.*

8. *Ibid.*

9. Adapted from the brochure, *Deaf-Blindness,* The Canadian National Institute for the Blind.

10. Adapted from the brochure, *Strokes – A Guide for the Family,* (c) American Heart Association, 7320 Greenville Ave., Dallas, TX 75231 . Canadian Heart Foundation, 1 Nicholas St., Ste. 1200, Ottawa, K1N 7B7.

11. Adapted from the book *Coping with Communication Disorders in Aging,* C. C. Publications, Inc., P. O. Box 23699, Tigard, Oregon.

12. Adapted from the article, "A Guide to Wheelchair Etiquette," Midwest Rehabilitation Institute of Covenant (formerly Shoitz) Medical Center, Waterloo, Iowa.

13. Adapted from the brochure, *Alzheimer's Disease, A Family Information Handbook,* Government of Canada, National Advisory Council on Aging.

NC PRESS LIMITED

HEALTHBOOKS/FAMILYBOOKS SERIES

HEALTHBOOKS-FAMILYBOOKS: A double series of new lifestyle books from NC Press Limited.

HEALTHBOOKS and FAMILYBOOKS are a series of new and updated NC Press books written for the concerned caregiver, professional health care worker, and lay person alike. Each of these titles is designed to provide the most up-to-date information on health and family matters in a pleasing to read style. Each book includes a resource list for further reading in related fields.

To this end, NC Press has engaged Dr. William (Bill) Weiss, M.D., C.C.F.P., P.Eng., as Editor-in-Chief.

Bill Weiss brings a wide medical and technical background to his editorial work including practical experience in neurology, emergency medicine, occupational and environmental medicine, and gerontology. He has also brought his engineering and computer background to the medical world through his consultancy on a variety of medical information systems and research projects in both the United States and Canada. Dr. Weiss is a columnist for *The Medical Post* and *Physicians Management Manuals.*

We want readers to be able to share these books with the same close friends with whom they share their personal health and family concerns. We invite you to write us with your comments and questions.

We welcome the opportunity to consider other non-technical books on innovations in healthcare delivery, women's health care, aging, cost and accessibility of health care, new frontiers in diagnosis and treatment, new technologies, occupational health, environmental concerns, immune system disorders, and health ethics.

Please forward your inquiries to:

HEALTHBOOKS-FAMILYBOOKS
NC Press Limited
260 Richmond St. W.
Suite 401
Toronto ON
M5V 1W5
CANADA

Order by mail

NC PRESS FAMILYBOOKS SERIES

Choices: For People Who Have A Terminal Illness, Their Families and Caregivers Harry van Bommel

From interviews with the dying and their caregivers, van Bommel provides excellent guidelines to encourage cooperation and communication within the family and between patient and caregiver. $12.95

Aging is a Family Affair: A Guide to Quality Visiting, Long-Term Care Facilities and You Wendy Thompson

Caring for older relatives can involve moving that person to an institution, sorting through a myriad of care options, and adjusting to changing family relationships. Here is a guide to help you understand and make the most of this time of change. $12.95

Love in the Blended Family: Falling in Love with a Package Deal Angela Neumann Clubb

For anyone who wants to understand step-motherhood and blended family life, here is realistic advice on learning to develop more honesty, trust and love in your family relationships. $12.95

Mother's Favourites compiled by Catherine Young

Explores the intimate relationship between mother and child. From the editor of the enormously successful Compleat Mother magazine, Mother's Favourites shares fresh hope, pleasure, grief, fear, wisdom, and laughter — the elements of life, from mother to mother. $12.95

Intuition: Success Strategies Judith Ennamorato

A refreshing look at intuitive thought, this book suggests how to recognize and develop intuitive capability to achieve success. $16.95

Getting High in Natural Ways: An Infobook for Young People of All Ages Nancy Levinson, Joanne Rocklin

If we understand what makes us feel good we can find our own ways to reach that feeling more often through creative and productive methods. $9.95

Midwifery is Catching Elanor Barrington

Covers and clarifies the complex issues surrounding midwifery • midwives and Canadian law • finding and selecting the right midwife • case histories • hospital and home birth • safety and medical opinion. $12.95

Coping with Death in the Family Dr. Gerald Schneiderman, M.D.

A common sense guide for lay persons and professionals on living with the loss of a loved one. $9.95

The Pre-School Craft Book Toy Martin

83 fully illustrated craft projects listing all materials, most of which can be found around the home. A wonderful solution to rainy afternoons! $6.95

The Stroll: Inner City Subcultures by John Davidson as told to Laird Stevens

Authentic stories about the game and the players involved in teenage prostitution. The harsh reality of drugs, the violence, the despair, and the dreams in the subcultures of the urban sex merchants, set aginst the backdrop of legal attempts to find answers. $9.95

ARE THERE NC PRESS BOOKS YOU WANT, BUT CANNOT FIND IN YOUR LOCAL BOOKSTORE?Use this handy order form.

FAMILYBooks:

____ copies of Choices:
Harry van Bommel, ISBN 1-55021-020-3 @ $12.95 ________

____ copies of Aging is a Family Affair: A Guide to Quality Visiting, Long-Term Care Facilities and You
Wendy Thompson, ISBN 1-55021-029-7 @ $12.95 ________

____ copies of Love in the Blended Family: Falling in Love with a Package Deal
Angela Neumann Clubb, ISBN 1-55021-023-8 @ $12.95 ________

____ copies of Mother's Favourites
Catherine Young, ISBN 1-55021-019-X @ $12.95 ________

____ copies of Intuition: Success Strategies
Judith Ennamorato, ISBN 0-920053-93-9 @ $16.95 ________

____ copies of Getting High in Natural Ways: An Infobook for Young People of All Ages
Nancy Levinson, Joanne Rocklin, ISBN 0-920053-81-5 @ $9.95 ________

____ copies of Midwifery is Catching
Eleanor Barrington, ISBN 0-920053-35-1 @ $12.95 ________

____ copies of Coping with Death in the Family
Dr. Gerald Schneiderman, M.D. ISBN 0-920053-21-1 @ $9.95 ________

____ copies of Pre-School Craft
Toy Martin, ISBN 0-920053-24-6 @ $6.95 ________

____ copies of The Stroll
Laird Stevens, ISBN 0-920053-65-3 @ $9.95 ________

Shipping and handling ____$2.00__

TOTAL $________

Check one:

☐ cheque payable to NC PRESS LIMITED
☐ VISA Number ____________________
☐ MasterCard Expires: ____/____ Issued: ____/____

Signature ________________________________

Name (please print) ________________________________

Address ________________________________

City ____________________ Prov ________ Postal Code ____________

Mail to:

NC Press Ltd., 260 Richmond St. W, Ste. 401, Toronto, ON, M5V 1W5
in USA: NC Press Ltd., 170 Broadway, Ste. 201, New York, NY 10038

Order by mail

NC PRESS HEALTHBOOKS SERIES

Intimacy: Living as a Woman After Cancer Jacquelyn Johnson

Brings a message of hope; women can begin to feel positively about their bodies and themselves after breast, gynecological, or other cancers, with a renewed sense of womanliness and wholeness. $12.95

Life Without End: The Transplant Story P.J. Houlihan

Demystifies the process of organ donation and transplantation to help the consumer make informed decisions and to make transplant professionals more accountable to those who bear the costs, financial or otherwise. $12.95

Terminal Shock: The Health Hazards of Video Display Terminals Bob DeMatteo

World wide survey of research on radiation, chemichal, ultrasound hazards and their control. $12.95

Explorer's Guide to Repetetive Strain Injuries Paul Brennan

A must resource for medical and legal specialists in occupational health and safety, assembly-line workers, computer keyboard users and typists. $ 9.95

Smoke in the Workplace Non-Smokers' Rights Association

A no-lose strategy for cleaning up the air at work. $9.95

The Citizens' Guide to Lead: Uncovering a Hidden Health Hazard Barbara Wallace and Kathy Cooper.

The definitive guide to reducing risk against this major urban health hazard. $12.95

PMS: Premenstrual Syndrome Gilda Berger

An infobook about teenage women encouraging a positive approach to understanding and easing menstrual difficulties. $9.95

Choice Cooking Canadian Diabetes Association

Simply the best all-round cookbook for diabetics ever written. $12.95

The Gluten-Free Diet Book Peter Rawcliffe and Ruth Rolph

Over 120 recipes showing how good gluten-free cooking can be for those with gluten sensitivities. $9.95

The Diabetics' Get Fit Book Jacki Winter

A complete home workout without routine written especially for diabetics. $9.95

Aquafit R.C.M.P.

Exercise for swimmers and non-swimmers to be performed in and around water. $14.95

TEENAGERS TALK ABOUT . . .

An NC Press series based on interviews with teenagers about the issues that concern them most.

The Face in the Mirror: Teenagers Talk About Adoption Marion Crook

Reveals in the words of teenagers how young people are dealing with the fact of their adoption, their complex relationships, and the many unanswered questions about their biological mothers. $9.95

The Face in the Mirror Video $29.95

Teenagers Talk About Suicide Marion Crook

Why do today's teens try suicide? What are some means for prevention. Marion Crook talks to young people who found the courage to go beyond their pain and share their experiences for the benefit of other teens. $9.95

ARE THERE NC PRESS BOOKS YOU WANT, BUT CANNOT FIND IN YOUR LOCAL BOOKSTORE? Use this handy order form.

HEALTHBooks:

____ copies of Intimacy: Living as a Woman After Cancer
Jacquelyn Johnson, ISBN 1-55021-025-4 @ $12.95 ________

____ copies of Life Without End: The Transplant Story
P.J. Houlihan, ISBN 1-55021-017-3 @ $12.95 ________

____ copies of Terminal Shock: The Health Hazards of Video Display Terminals
Bob DeMatteo, ISBN 0-920053-87-4 @ $12.95 ________

____ copies of Explorer's Guide to Repetitive Strain Injuries
Paul Brennan, ISBN 9589494-0-9 @ $9.95 ________

____ copies of Smoke in the Workplace
Non-Smokers' Rights Assoc., ISBN 0-920053-75-0 @ $9.95 ________

____ copies of The Citizens' Guide to Lead: Uncovering a Hidden Health Hazard
Barbara Wallace, Kathy Cooper, ISBN 0-920053-92-0 @ $12.95 ________

____ copies of PMS: Premenstrual Syndrome
Gilda Berger, ISBN 0-920053-77-7 @ $9.95 ________

____ copies of Choice Cooking
Canadian Diabetes Assoc., ISBN 919601-69-3 @ $12.95 ________

____ copies of The Gluten-Free Diet Book
Peter Rawcliffe and Ruth Rolph, ISBN 0-920053-19-X @ $9.95 ________

____ copies of The Diabetics' Get Fit Book
Jacki Winter, ISBN 0-920053-42-4 @ $9.95 ________

____ copies of Aquafit
R.C.M.P., ISBN 0-920053-39-4 @ $14.95 ________

TEENAGERS TALK ABOUT . . .

____ copies of The Face in the Mirror
Marion Crook, ISBN 0-920053-67-X @ $9.95 ________

____ copies of The Face in the Mirror Video
Beta: 1-55021-028-9, VHS:1-55021-033-3 @ $29.95 ________

____ copies of Teenagers Talk About Suicide
Marion Crook, ISBN 1-55021-013-0 @ $9.95 ________

Shipping and handling $2.00

TOTAL $________

Check one:

☐ cheque payable to NC PRESS LIMITED
☐ VISA Number ________________ Expires: ____/____ Issued: ____/____
☐ MasterCard

Signature ______________________________

Name (please print) ______________________________

Address ______________________________

City ______________ Prov ________ Postal Code ______________

Mail to:

NC Press Ltd., 260 Richmond St. W, Ste. 401, Toronto, ON, M5V 1W5
in USA: NC Press Ltd., 170 Broadway, Ste. 201, New York, NY 10038